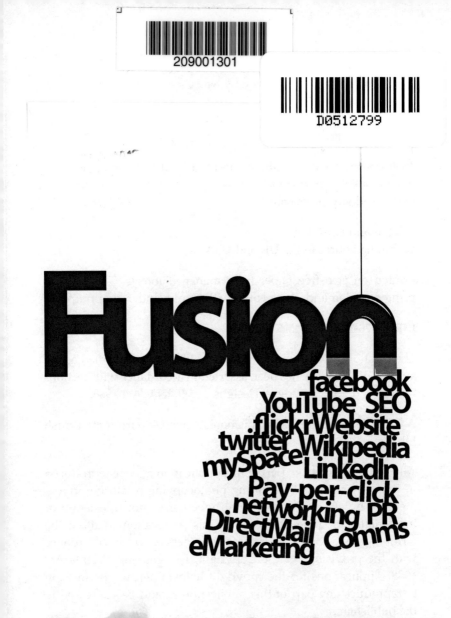

Fusion

facebook
YouTube SEO
flickr Website
twitter Wikipedia
mySpace LinkedIn
Pay-per-click
networking PR
DirectMail Comms
eMarketing

The new way of marketing

David Taylor & David Miles

Cover design and book design by Neil Coe

First published in 2011

Ecademy Press
48 St Vincent Drive, St Albans, Herts AL1 5SJ
info@ecademy-press.com
www.ecademy-press.com

Printed and bound by:
Lightning Source in the UK and USA

Printed on acid-free paper from managed forests. This book is
printed on demand, so no copies will be remaindered or pulped.

ISBN 978-1-907722-35-6

The right of David Taylor and David Miles to be identified as the
authors of this work has been asserted in accordance with sections
77 and 78 of the Copyright, Designs and Patents Act 1988.

A CIP catalogue record for this book is available from the British
Library.

Dedications

David Taylor

To Bernie Saunders for helping me learn to write, Joy Moon
for teaching me about marketing, Tim Rylatt for giving me the
original idea for the book, and of course my wife for her ability to
put up with my ways.

David Miles

To Dad for giving me a love of words, and to Jane for support
and forbearance beyond the call of duty.

Acknowledgements

In addition to our families and clients, the authors would like to thank the following people who have, knowingly or unknowingly, helped them to write this book:

Mindy Gibbins-Klein, Kent Rhodes, Ben Howe, Howard Graham, Laura Hurren, Graham Seymour, Ian Cass, Ian Purvis, Chris Gridley, and Hilary Mackelden.

Contents

Introduction

Mankind is now entering completely uncharted territory. For the first time in history, individuals, organisations, businesses, charities and pressure groups can publicise themselves without relying on third parties to publish their work, be it via newspapers, television or even propaganda.

The development of the internet over the past twenty years, coupled with the recent appearance of social networking sites such as Twitter, MySpace, Facebook and YouTube has completely revolutionised the way we all communicate with the world around us.

Using an easily accessible and cheap 'smartphone', it is possible for an individual to take a photo, or even a video, and post it to the other side of the world in seconds. Alternatively an aspiring recording artist can set up a page on a social networking site and use this to advertise themselves to a potential global audience for free.

Many people – especially, but not exclusively, the under 30s or so-called Generation Y – totally understand this new world order. Millions of people around the world have some form of social networking account and the internet has become the first port of call for anyone wishing to access information.

Yet for large swathes of the population in Europe, the internet is still seen as a mystical place inhabited solely by geeks, youngsters and pornographers; blogs are updated on a daily basis by people with nothing better to do, while social networking sites are for kids and bored celebrities.

Our aim with this book is to reach out to all these 'non believers', demystify how the internet works and show how social media can be a real force for change, not only in society but also in the way we market ourselves in the new media age.

At the same time, we want to show people in a wide range of fields, from small business owners to marketing managers and from charity directors to local authority communications teams, that there are so many opportunities to be had from using online technology in an intelligent way.

Gone is the era of simply throwing money at marketing and hoping it will work. In these cash-strapped times, it is vital that every penny of investment in marketing is well spent. At the same time, people need to recognise that using their brain instead of their bank account will yield better results.

Chapter 1
The world has changed

Technology has revolutionised the way we consume the media

Since the beginning of time, mankind has communicated. In the Stone Age it was by hand gestures, primitive speech and drawings on cave walls. Over the next few hundred years, the only real progress was the invention of paper and the writing instruments to go with it.

The invention of the printing press by Caxton in the 15th Century helped us take a quantum leap forward by making the written word accessible to more than just a few privileged monks or royal families. For the first time, many more people – artists, writers, scholars – had access to information and this, we believe, had a key role to play in the flowering of The Renaissance in Europe.

Moving forward, once newspapers appeared on the scene in the early 17th Century, even more people had access to news and information.

Of course, things really hotted up in the early 19th Century with the invention in fairly quick succession of the telegraph, telephone, gramophone and wireless – the age of media 'for the masses' was slowly dawning.

However, the late 20th Century will be seen as the great era of mass media with magazines, movies, television, VHS, cassettes, cable and satellite TV, CDs and DVDs all vying for our attention. It is the period from 1945 until the mid 1990s which can now be seen as a 'golden age', when large swathes of the population read the same papers, watched the same films, listened to the same music and enjoyed the same hit shows on television.

Anyone over the age of 35 can still remember a time when top rated TV shows would command audiences in excess of 20 million or when a record would have to sell several hundred thousand copies to reach Number One in the charts. Newspapers too would routinely be read by a majority of the population at local, regional and national level.

Even now, we still have the mass media – shows like the X-Factor, Britain's Got Talent and soap operas still pull in the TV viewers while blockbuster films still command enormous audiences.

However, every major form of communication in the Western World has experienced a decline in the past 15 or so years – book and record sales, newspaper readership, TV and film audiences have all seen a slump. All because of something invented by the British scientist Tim Berners-Lee in 1989. That something was the World Wide Web, which brought the use of the internet to the masses (**http://bit.ly/cwF1dH**).

With the advent of broadband technology and the production of superfast microprocessors over the second decade of its short public life, the internet has come into its own and is providing the backdrop to a revolution which surpasses even that created by the invention of the printing press or the television.

The development of interactive websites and web logs (or blogs as we now commonly call them) presaged a further technological development – so-called social networking sites which we now refer to as an entirely new form of communications: social media.

Now, for the first time in our history, ordinary people have the power to broadcast their thoughts, images and films to the rest of the world. And it is this democratisation of the means of media production which has truly revolutionised how mankind accesses information.

If that is what can be achieved by individuals, think of the range of possibilities for business and the implications for marketing and public relations. For example, why pay for expensive advertising or PR campaigns when you could simply replace them with a well-written blog combined with elements of search engine optimisation and pay-per-click advertising?

Video also has the power to transform your brand and make websites three-dimensional marketing tools which give a far greater depth of information than traditional marketing has ever been able to do – without spending thousands of pounds that is.

Social media too can extend your target audience exponentially as well as helping to build your brand in a way that only huge advertising budgets would once have done.

The key thing is not to be afraid or dismissive of these new technologies but to try to understand them and see how they can apply to your business or organisation. After all, many of these new marketing tools are completely free!

Emergence of Generation Y or the Facebook Generation

The generation of people growing up in this new media environment is the one which is most directly affected by it and it is they who will shape the world in which we live.

Known as the Facebook Generation or Generation 'Y' (the children of people born in the 1960s and 70s, who are known as Generation X), these teenagers and 20-somethings view the world in an entirely different way from their parents.

Less trusting of authority and more likely to take risks, these youngsters have never known a time without computers or mobile phones, while the majority will have been accessing the internet from an early age. Texting, gaming, instant messaging, emails and virtual reality are all taken for granted.

Generation Y (**http://en.wikipedia.org/wiki/Generation_Y**) has also witnessed the emergence of multi-channel television, catering for almost all tastes. TV sets are now dotted around houses with individual family members watching programmes in their own rooms.

The plethora of gadgets available means that these youngsters have a huge variety of ways to occupy their time. It's not uncommon for teenagers to be talking to friends on a mobile, whilst listening to their iPods and sending emails.

The consequence of this multi-skilling, as well as the development of texting and the huge availability of media channels, is that attention spans are much shorter. Like magpies, this generation will flit from one thing to another. It is unsurprising then that sites like Twitter (**www.twitter.com**) have proved so popular. Why read a whole article when it can be distilled into just 140 characters?

Trying to employ traditional marketing techniques, then, will just not work with this generation. They don't really read newspapers (certainly not local ones), they spend little time on the terrestrial channels and apart from BBC Radio 1 (**www.bbc.co.uk/radio1**) as well as possibly some of the larger commercial stations such as XFM (**www.xfm.co.uk**) or Absolute Radio (**www.absoluteradio.co.uk**), they don't listen to mainstream radio.

So where do they get their information from? The simple answer is that it could be from a wide variety of sources: from social media sites at home or (more commonly now) via their mobile phones to blogs, adverts on Playstation or X-Box games, or satellite TV and radio. In fact a study out in the United States at the start of 2011 showed that the internet is now the main national and international news source for people aged 18 to 29 (source Mashable – **http://on.mash.to/f2wKxk**).

For many people (young and old alike), the first thing they will do when they get up is to check their Facebook page – in much the same way as people will have traditionally read the morning paper or tuned into the radio. This represents a quantum shift in behaviour which is slowly filtering down into all areas of business.

At the same time however, there has been a substantial knock-on effect across all the other age groups. The largest group of people to go online in the past couple of years has been Generation X themselves, now growing older 'disgracefully' and being labelled as 'silver surfers'.

This is the first generation for whom age is no barrier and they are a huge force to be reckoned with. For them, ordering products online, searching on Google for information and booking flights are now almost second-nature. So, you may then not be surprised to learn that one in four people on the internet is over 50 (**http://bit.ly/c4GlXB**) and many of these people are happily adapting to the changing media landscape.

Take a moment to think about how many people do you know in their 60s who are on Facebook? How many own a Blackberry or an iPhone? And how many still read a broadsheet newspaper cover-to-cover every day of the week?

You may be surprised by the answers, if not now then in the coming one, two or five years as the revolution gathers pace. The way people access the media is constantly changing but is your marketing changing to reflect this? When was the last time you took a close look at how your target audiences access information and are you making incorrect assumptions based on people's age or background?

Of course another huge step forward in the past few years has been the advent of mobile internet and the plethora of applications (apps). This has meant that the personal computer has metamorphosed into a tiny handheld device onto which you can download any number of clever programs. At the last count, there were over 300,000 for the iPhone alone and these can do anything from telling you the time of the next train home to helping you cook your evening meal.

Many companies and organisations are now commissioning their own apps, as simplified versions of their websites. For instance eBay, Amazon and IKEA all have their own apps, making it easier than ever to buy their products – even when you are on the move.

Traditional media has lost its pre-eminence

So, where does this leave our traditional media? Certainly, we now live in an age where there is huge competition for people's attention and everything moves at such a rapid pace. In some ways, media such as newspapers, magazines and local radio all seem like anachronisms in this modern, social media era.

While it is true that many local newspapers have had to close or merge, circulations of all the major national newspapers are falling year-on-year and the TV audiences on terrestrial channels are nothing like they were even in the 1980s, it would be wrong to prophesy the imminent demise of traditional media. After all, nearly 11 million people still read national newspapers daily.

In fact, many outlets are adapting. The BBC now has one of the world's most read websites (**www.bbc.co.uk**), most national papers have invested in their own websites, local newspapers are evolving to take into account their digital readership and the advent of digital radio (**www.getdigitalradio.com**) has given even local stations a far greater potential audience.

However, as we said earlier in the book, what has been termed as the Golden Age of mass media is over. This is rapidly being replaced by an enormous amount of niche marketplaces – a mass of niches if you will.

For example, a generation ago, a typical 40-something married father of two, may have settled down to watch the BBC or ITV with his family, hoping there may be something that suited one of his interests – be it football, tennis, cooking, Westerns or historical documentaries. Similarly, as a classic rock fan, he might have tuned into one of the main radio stations and been satisfied if a small proportion of the music played was by one of his favourite bands like The Who, Rolling Stones or Led Zeppelin.

Fast forward to the 2010s and there are entire TV channels dedicated to any one of these interests, while stations such as Planet Rock (**www.planetrock.com**) ensure Pete Townsend, Keith Richards or Jimmy Page can play uninterrupted into the night!

Furthermore, there are now websites to cater for every known (and probably as-yet unknown) predilection, all at the click of a mouse or, increasingly, the press of a button or the touch of a screen on a smartphone.

It is the internet which has made the biggest difference to our media consumption. There are billions of pages of information in every conceivable language, accessible 24/7 from a host of different platforms (PCs, games consoles, iPads, phones) and ever changing to match the tastes of consumers.

Rather than compete with this – which is nigh on impossible – the traditional media is making itself complementary. TV programmes now have their own websites and social networking channels, while newspapers incorporate multimedia into their online editions. Even this book, one of the most traditional forms of communications, is littered with links to web pages and is itself available as a digital download.

Traditional media is certainly not going to disappear overnight, especially when we have an aging population who will always prefer print over digital. Printed newspapers may have some form of a future, though, like vinyl records, they are likely to occupy a niche rather than a mass market. Yet with the introduction of the iPad and other tablet-like devices, printing news onto paper may actually die out completely – something that even the likes of Rupert Murdoch are contemplating. Indeed, he believes that the iPad is the way forward (see **http://bit.ly/fAJaE2**) and is investing in new technology to go on it – check out the Times app for the iPad and you'll see what we mean.

Whatever the pace of change though and the proportion of your target market who are young or old, it is vital that all organisations – public or private sector alike – prepare for this changing environment. Doing nothing is simply not an option, nor is pretending that the whole 'internet and social media thing' is just another phase and that traditional ways of marketing will somehow win out over technology.

The impact on business

Clearly, this revolution taking place is already starting to have a major effect on how businesses communicate with their target audiences. Instead of relying on traditional 'outbound' marketing (a strategy that focuses on finding customers by building brand awareness through advertising and promotion), we are moving to a new model of 'inbound' marketing – this model focuses on getting found by customers. To find out more on this, read Brian Halligan's blog – **http://bit.ly/hysZve** – which looks in detail at the differences between the two forms of marketing.

Yet we believe that the majority of organisations in the UK – whether they are large corporations, SMEs, charities or pressure groups –

simply don't grasp the enormity of the changes taking place in the media. Therefore, many either have marketing strategies which are way out of date (still very much 'outbound') or are attempting to deal with the emerging new media in a piecemeal fashion without really understanding it.

For example, a couple of years ago a colleague from a property marketing agency was handling the PR for a residential property development in Reading. The developer had done their homework on the target market and therefore the advertising and PR were aimed at people in their 20s and 30s.

For some reason, the developer decided to focus on the local press, spending hundreds of pounds on adverts and courting the local newspapers. The marketing agency questioned the developer about why they were doing this when it was unlikely that any of their target audience would be reading these publications, and they advised them that they were wasting their money.

The agency recommended spending the money instead on a blog which could be added to the developer's website and regularly updated with news, information about the development and interesting events happening in Reading. They also advised them to add social media profiles to the website as these would accurately cater for the 20- and 30-somethings who were the scheme's target market.

A similar strategy was employed in London by developer Marldon on their **www.67turnmillstreet.com** development, and proved to be very successful. The website for that development is a classic example of how residential property marketing campaigns *should* be run and the result was that all the properties sold with a bare minimum of traditional advertising spending.

This is quite a rare example, though, and many people simply want to use the tried and trusted methods of marketing. As we see it, one clear problem is that the majority of people in management in the UK and Europe are in their 40s and 50s and will have long track records in their industries or sectors. Many will be loathe to embrace new technology or simply dismiss it as just a passing phase. This will be especially true in business to business sectors which still rely firmly on traditional marketing methods.

Another issue is that as a result of the recent economic downturn, many businesses and organisations have reduced spending on marketing or have stopped it all together, thereby leaving themselves unable to compete properly. Websites only have a shelf life of three years and most companies' online presence will have been out-of-date even prior to the recession.

The result is that the vast majority of organisations simply haven't grasped the importance of having a strong online presence and their websites reflect this. Nor can they see that the far-reaching consequences of the media revolution we are currently experiencing will help to shape the workplaces, high streets and even population centres of the future.

Already, organisations such as the Federation of Corporate Real Estate (**www.fedcre.com**) are looking at whether it will be feasible to have large office buildings in the future, when flexible work styles have been adopted by employees. Some roles will have to change – notably in marketing, PR, human resources and customer relations – while there will be new roles emerging such as social media managers and web analytics statisticians.

With so many employees using social media sites and eventually incorporating them into marketing strategies, the days of banning their use at work will have to come to an end (most employees can access the sites on their phones anyway) and proper guidelines will need to be implemented.

Already on the high street, many independent shops are finding it hard to compete with the larger chains while paying expensive business rates and rentals. However, with a well defined online marketing strategy, it will be less important to have a physical shop presence and crucial to have an online 'shop window'. Therefore, many town centre retailers will be free to take cheaper and less high profile locations or even do away with having a shop at all.

An excellent example of this is Woolworths. A common sight on high streets up and down the country since 1909, the chain at one time had over 1,000 stores. However, increasing competition from supermarkets, Argos and online websites meant it was no longer viable and it ceased trading in 2009. Yet, it has been reborn as an online shop itself and **www.woolworths.co.uk** now sells many of the same goods as its old-fashioned predecessor did, yet without the overheads.

Of course, one of the world's most successful retailers has taken this to a whole new dimension. Amazon was founded in 1995 and has been in the UK (**www.amazon.co.uk**) since 1998. Its entire model is based on having no physical outlets, a powerful website and minimal advertising budget. The result is that is has grown to be one of the largest retailers in the UK and, from its beginnings as a website selling primarily books and music, it now sells thousands of different lines.

Not only that, but through its Amazon Marketplace programme, the company allows other retailers to use its website to sell their goods. Therefore, a small book shop in, say Barnsley, could market all its stock on Amazon, in the same way as individuals would sell something on another internet success story eBay (**www.ebay.co.uk**). Amazon would of course take a commission but the shop would dramatically increase its potential customer base from South Yorkshire to the entire globe.

This means that many struggling retailers, who would otherwise have found it difficult to stay in business, now have an online outlet which, at a stroke, makes them far more viable.

With the emergence of a potentially new type of flexible working, meaning less need for commuting and large office buildings, combined with a different approach to retailing, it is possible to foresee an entirely new landscape in the UK where small village shops can once more become viable, rural communities get a new lease of life and town centres become the preserve of leisure pursuits such as pubs, bars and restaurants.

Of course, much of this depends on the access to high speed broadband, which is as important to the future of the this country as the development of the canals and railways was in the 18/19th

Centuries, along with the construction of the motorway network in the 20th Century.

The Government recently announced plans for everyone to have access to high speed broadband by 2015 (**http://bbc.in/glaZX5**) with the provision of digital 'hubs' in every community. This will mean the country is properly equipped to compete in the digital age but it will rely on both Government and private sector funding.

This does illustrate, though, just how important the internet now is to our economy and society as a whole. Clearly politicians want the United Kingdom to be as competitive as possible in the global economy. Now it is down to businesses to grasp the nettle and do the same with their digital and marketing strategies.

Suggested action plan

- How well do you understand the new media landscape? To get an idea about how marketing is changing, type a few phrases into Google such as *'online marketing'*, *'new rules of marketing and PR'*, or *'social media revolution'* to see what you get. If the whole thing scares you then, if nothing else, hopefully this book will set your mind at rest!

- How well do you know your target audiences and how do they access the media? If you are unsure, you might like to try surveying them to find out. Chances are that if you asked them even five years ago, the answers you get today will be very different. If they have changed the way they access information, shouldn't you be changing your marketing to reflect this?

- Have a look at some major organisations' websites and see how technologically advanced they are. You could still use many of these innovations yourself though, as the cost of new technology is falling all the time.

- Speak to people under 25 and try to understand the world from their perspective. What do they use social networking sites for and what traditional media do they access?

- Look at your own town or city. How has it changed over the past five years and is it equipped to deal with the changes brought by the social media revolution? You may like to speak to fellow businesses at networking forums to gauge their thoughts. If there are web designers in these groups, seek them out and find out the latest thinking.

Chapter 2

Ensure your website *is* your marketing strategy

A little bit of history

The internet is, then, the pre-eminent communications tool of our age and has rapidly become a necessity, not only for business but also for almost every aspect of our daily life. Therefore, rather than being one of your marketing tools, your website *is*, for all intents and purposes, your marketing strategy.

To understand a little more about it, though, we have to go back a decade or so to see how internet marketing has evolved. The key driver throughout has been technological development, much of it in the United States. This gave rise to the Dotcom boom of the late 1990s.

This mini revolution was driven by the overwhelming demand for corporations, businesses and brands to get an online identity – a digital footprint, so to speak. As the invention of radio and television radically increased the audiences that could be reached earlier in the 20th Century, so too did the evolution in the technology to build websites at the end of the Millennium. Initially first-adopters such as the retail sector, then the wider business population, started to grasp the possibilities offered by this new marketing medium.

Known now as Web 1.0, many of these websites served simply as online advertisements for the product or organisation they were meant to be promoting. Mostly static and with large numbers of pages, they barely differed from printed brochures or adverts. They were often seen as an after-thought, with lots of firms jumping onto the internet bandwagon without having given any proper thought to how this would fit in with their current marketing strategy.

Over ten years on, and for an overwhelming number of organisations, this is what their website continues to do. Even more shockingly, almost a fifth of small firms in the UK still do not have a website, according to new research by the Forum of Private Business (**http://ht.ly/19swZK**). That's akin to having a shop in a prime location with no door, no shop window and nothing to advertise what it is you sell!

Technology is now moving forward at such a rapid pace though. We're now in the Web 2.0 (**http://en.wikipedia.org/wiki/Web_2.0**) age and many observers are even talking about Web 3.0 – just type web 3.0 into Google to see what you get. Yet, so many organisations are lagging further and further behind, not only because of the financial pressures brought on by the recession but also because of fear of the unknown.

Imagine, if you like, going back to the Dotcom era of 1999/2000 just over a decade ago. No digital music players, mobile phones that could only be used to speak on and send text messages, no mobile internet, and PCs with barely 1GB of memory and slow processors.

Think of the amazing technological advances that have been made during this time: the invention of the iPod (October 2001), the introduction of 3G technology in 2001 which then heralded the advent of a mobile internet, and the introduction of smartphones such as Blackberries and iPhones. Many of these portable devices have processors which are faster and far more efficient than many PCs while the memory available has risen exponentially to cope with all the new applications.

If technology has moved forward at such a rapid pace, why would it still be OK to have a website developed during the 1990s? It would be like having a modern car but deciding to fit it with an engine from the 1980s – it would work but, compared to what's around now, it simply wouldn't have the performance or efficiency.

The key stumbling block is cost. Many companies would have shelled out thousands of pounds for what were seen at the time to be bespoke, top-of-the-range websites. Now many of these are hopelessly out-of-date but there is a general level of anxiety about investing in new websites. Costs have dropped dramatically with many simple sites being built for around £2,000. If you assume that this will then last you three years, that only works out as a monthly investment of £56, which is pretty reasonable when compared with other marketing costs.

Your website – a metaphorical window on the world

With recent advances in website technology such as the development of social networking sites, blogs, wikis, file-sharing and web applications (now known as 'apps'), the humble Web 1.0 or basic website has been transformed from a rather one-dimensional form of peripheral marketing into something completely different.

In its place is something that most people in the year 2000 could only dream about – a multi-functional, two-way, easily updated communications tool that allows the world to see your brand/ product/service in all its glory.

Video feeds, interactive forums, rolling news and e-commerce functions are all part and parcel of modern websites. Just take a quick look at the most popular sites in the UK such as **www.bbc.co.uk**, **www.ebay.co.uk**, **www.amazon.co.uk** or **www.tesco.com** to see how advanced websites can be.

A great example of how to use the internet really effectively is the porn industry. We all know that sex sells, but never was this truer than in the modern age. Producers of pornography have always been at the forefront of technology, whether it was using Super 8 film, video tape, DVDs or multi-layered websites. Much of what is now commonplace today – interactive websites, embedded video, e-commerce – was pioneered by people wanting to sell sex.

Of course, pornographers and large businesses can afford to lavish millions of pounds on these sites but the same technology is there to be used by smaller organisations and it *is* now affordable.

Gone too are the days when companies had to pay huge monthly retainers to web designers just to have a few words or pictures altered or added to a site. Free software such as Wordpress (**www.wordpress.org**) is making websites as easy to content manage as your own personal Facebook page.

The prize of course is to gain exposure to a potentially global audience of customers, or at the very least, the greatest possible proportion of your target markets. Even if you don't rely on your website to generate your sales leads, it is there to back up all your other marketing and to leverage your brand.

Let's take for example a small record shop in East Sussex which specialises in selling vinyl records from the 1960s, 70s and 80s. Passing traffic is likely to be very light, while few people from more than a twenty mile radius are likely to want to visit the shop.

However, with a correctly functioning website and clever marketing around it including social media, the shop-front becomes virtual and the proprietor can communicate with people from all over the world. Also, as we mentioned earlier, by marketing its products on eBay and Amazon, the shop can increase its audience even further.

Incidentally, the record shop is a classic example of a once mass market which still survives as a niche. For more information go to **www.indierecordshop.org**, which is using the internet to help sell this now obsolescent product (something which we believe newspapers will also eventually become).

Websites such as the online auction site eBay have done a great deal to bring to even the smallest retailer the potential for trading internationally. For example, it is now perfectly possible to list a CD for sale on eBay's UK site (**www.ebay.co.uk**) from where it then goes on to reach a global audience via **www.ebay.com**. Just recently, this led to one of the authors selling an album to someone in Tasmania.

Dating websites (rather cleaner versions than the porn ones!) show similar disregard to international boundaries and people can effectively market themselves on a personal level to a worldwide audience.

At the same time, any organisation that needs to attract a global client base such as hotels, visitor attractions, private schools or universities, can now do so without having to shell out enormous amounts of money on international advertising campaigns or affiliate marketing.

One example is the boutique Brighton hotel, Sea Spray (**www.seaspraybrighton.co.uk**). They had visits to their website from 143 different countries over a one year period. Think about it – what an incredible opportunity to leverage their brand. This is just one illustration of how websites have opened up vast opportunities for organisations – our job is to help you grasp them.

One way to do this is to put yourself into the shoes of a potential visitor to your website. Even better, ask your customers or friends to give you their honest opinion about it. Bearing in mind that your website is your shop window on the world, does it do your brand justice or is it more of a millstone around your neck?

It is incredible the number of organisations we speak to who, when asked about their website, reply: "Oh, don't look at it, it's dreadful!" Others, when looking at their website objectively realise that is doesn't reflect who they are or what they do.

This is like trying to sell wedding dresses from a tatty, dingy basement rather than in a bright, spacious showroom complete with comfy chairs and filter coffee. Or advertising yourself as a gardener when in reality you are garden designer. Which would you rather have?

We like to think that your website should be able to do as good a job at selling your brand as you can. If yours doesn't, you might need to take a long, hard look at what it is saying.

Get it right and all other forms of marketing work better

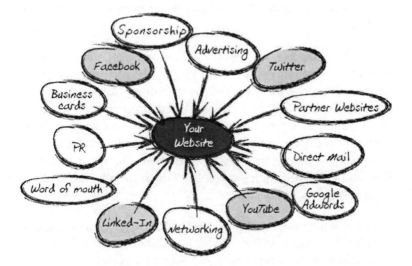

The diagram above shows the importance of your website and how it forms the core of your marketing strategy, with everything else acting as a means of driving people to the site. Get your website right and all your other forms of marketing will work better. Get it wrong and it is like building a house on sand, no matter how well crafted the rest of your marketing strategy is.

This illustration can almost apply to any organisation, whether you are a psychotherapist, local authority, specialist greengrocer or a multi-national company. Of course, some of the circles in the diagram will be more important than others, but the principle is the same – driving as much traffic to your website as possible.

Note too, how many of these marketing tools are free. Out of the thirteen key forms of marketing shown here, over half are FREE! As well as the social networking sites (you could of course add in any of the other 200+ sites which exist), partner websites, word of mouth and business cards will cost you next to nothing, while networking can deliver you an incredibly good return on your investment. We'll be focusing on these in more detail later on.

It might be an idea to apply this diagram to your own marketing.

Where does your website currently fit and how effective are your direct mail, advertising, public relations, etc? Good marketing has always been integrated but this has never been so true as in the 21st Century.

Take this example. A couple of years ago, the property marketing company Adventis (**www.adventisproperty.co.uk**) was handling the PR for a couple of housing associations who were looking to sell part-buy/part-rent properties. One had a well-optimised, interesting microsite (a self contained website accessible independently or via the main website) for the specific development they were looking to market. The other relied on their old-fashioned, generic website which didn't even make it clear that they sold houses.

Press coverage was duly obtained in The Metro (**www.metro.co.uk**), the ideal target market for housing associations with its 1million+ readership and young demographic. Each of the two developments had equal space on a one-page special affordable feature, including a write-up and photo. The key thing, though, was that they didn't include any contact details so readers would have had to search for them on Google, Bing, etc.

The article was published and a week later Adventis checked with both organisations to see how many leads had filtered through to their sales teams. The first housing association had seen a phenomenal response from people who had easily found the development's microsite by going into search engines. They were absolutely thrilled with the huge number of sales leads that had been generated and all the units were got rid of with the minimum of advertising and marketing spend.

All was very different over at the second housing association. Because their website was so poor, readers had been unable to find any details on the development on Google, Bing or Yahoo and had therefore hit a dead end. The result? Not a single sales lead. So all the money spent on PR and advertising had been a waste. Their metaphorical 'house' had collapsed into the sand. To make matters worse, the head office of the organisation simply did not see the website as a viable sales tool. For the sales team, this was akin to fighting with both hands tied behind their back.

So the quality of your website really does affect all your other forms of marketing. Take a very old fashioned way of promoting your product or brand – the humble business card. You can spend time with a potential customer at a trade show, explaining what you do before handing over your card. The first thing they will do is take a look at your website, either once they get back to their office, or more usually these days, on their phone or Blackberry.

If you have a cracking website, your sales pitch will be backed up by a quality marketing tool, thereby assisting you in converting a lead into a sale. However, if your site is not up to the mark, your face-to-face sales pitch may have been in vain. Go through all the other forms of marketing and the same is true. They are all designed to drive traffic through to your website, so it had better be good.

Another great way to advertise not only your website but also your social media pages and even your personal brand (via LinkedIn), is using your email signature. It is still surprising the amount of people who just have their phone and fax numbers listed. With the help of hyperlinks to specific pages, you can give your customers easy access to all the information they may need from you or your company.

Providing the foundation for everything you do

Instead of being a peripheral marketing tool then, your website should form the very heart of any marketing strategy. This is why it is so vital to make sure your website is the very best that you can afford and your brand is well represented.

This has implications not just for your marketing but for many other areas of the business such as internal communications, HR, customer relations, media relations and stakeholder communications. None of these can be treated in isolation any more – that's why there needs to be a clear, thought-out strategy.

We call this 'fusion' marketing where everything is inter-linked. That's why it is so important that you are very clear about exactly how to represent your brand online – or indeed how you protect your brand, under certain circumstances.

This is where social media comes into the equation. As we will see in the next chapter, rather than something which is done independently or on an ad hoc basis, websites such as Twitter, Facebook, LinkedIn, YouTube (and to a certain extent even eBay, Amazon and a large host of other sites) are merely yet another way to build your brand and drive traffic to your website.

Again, to use an example from one of the authors' websites: over a year of business, 12% of traffic to the 2010media website came via Twitter, 3% from Facebook and 2% from LinkedIn. All of these were completely free and took only a negligible amount of time to update.

However, we often meet people who are very active on social media, tweeting on an hourly basis or updating Facebook pages constantly – but for what purpose? Like any form of marketing, it must be cleverly targeted and representative of your target audiences.

Furthermore, as we highlighted earlier, if your website is no good, no matter how much activity there is on social networks, it will be far less effective than if your site were great.

Helping you sell products or leverage your brand

Of course, depending on the area of business you are in – business to business, business to consumer, charity or professional services – the role your website will have is very different.

A small garden nursery in rural Herefordshire which relies almost totally on their website is very different from a City law firm which merely wishes to enhance its online reputation or a charity that wants to educate as well as raise funds.

So let's look at the first example. A quick search on Google for 'garden nurseries Herefordshire' comes up with the Herefordshire section of the online portal **www.thegardeningwebsite.co.uk**. Looking down the list of nurseries, many don't have websites (inexcusable in this day and age), some have basic ones with just text, while some are in line with modern 'fusion' marketing.

The company that stands out head and shoulders over the others though is Ornamental Tree Nurseries of Kingsland who have the website **www.ornamental-trees.co.uk**. This is a proper, well put-together and up-to-date e-commerce site. They are also on Facebook and Twitter, giving them even more chances of successfully leveraging their brand online. Clearly, any marketing they choose to do, whether it be traditional or online, has the greatest chance of success. In this example then, the vast majority of their sales are going to come via their website.

Of course, another advantage of relying on a good website is that it really doesn't matter where you trade from – be it the middle of a field, down a country lane, or on a trading estate. Low overheads and not having to maintain an expensive 'shop front' for customers mean that costs can be kept to a minimum.

At the other end of the business spectrum is the City law firm. Here, a large amount of new business leads will still come via word of mouth or personal recommendation so in this case the website has a rather different role to play. Instead of 'selling' directly, it is there to enhance the brand and give the firm the best chance of success when given a referral. In essence, it is not just about turning warm leads into hot ones but making sure that hot leads don't go cold because the website simply isn't good enough.

Also, if someone does decide to search for your area of business on Google or any other search engine, how will you differentiate yourself from your competitors when in essence, you all do very much the same thing? This is where brand and personality are so important.

To put this into a real world context, being on the first page of Google is like being in Strictly Come Dancing (**www.facebook.com/bbcstrictly**) with nine of your most direct competitors, all of whom are as competent as you at the Tango or Quickstep (services you provide). In front of you are various judges (your potential customers), who are all eager to mark you on your dancing (how well your brand is represented online). However, to win, you have to make the right first impression (decent home page) and put on a better performance than the others (have a better website).

Try this out for yourself. Wherever you are in the country type the name of your town or area, along with the professional service you require, into a search engine. Up will come a list of companies. Next, compare each of the websites listed. You'll be amazed at how they vary.

Now try it out using search terms relevant to your own website. Hopefully you'll be on the first page of Google (if not, we will come onto how to fix this in a later chapter) and you can then see how you come across compared to your competitors.

Charities have a different use for their websites. Not only are they trying to educate people about what it is they do, but very often they are a primary means of fundraising, along with having an e-commerce element for any merchandise they want to sell.

Here again, for any charity to be credible and get its message across as effectively as possible, the website must be able to act as a primary source of information – whether for stakeholders, donors or the general public.

Like it or not, the truth is that, increasingly, people are less willing to pick up the phone to find out information. So the more user-friendly, informative and branded you can make your website the better, even if someone has recommended you.

Suggested action plan

- Is your website Web 2.0 or does it look completely dated when compared with your competitors and modern sites? Draw up a list of ten main competitors and see what their online presence is like. Even if you are well optimised and can be found easily on search engines, the chances are that if their sites are better, you WILL lose business.

- Is your website at the heart of your marketing strategy or is it more of an afterthought? Your marketing strategy MUST be built around your website and all strategic decisions regarding investment in marketing will be based on having a site that performs to the best of its ability.

- Have you analysed how well your website performs or studied the effectiveness of your marketing using Google Analytics (more on this in Chapter 5)? Chances are that if you don't know how well your site is performing, you may well be wasting money on marketing.

- How is your brand or company viewed online? Ask some leading clients and colleagues to rate the effectiveness of your website. You may get some interesting answers. You may even think about running a survey of your customers so they can rate all aspects of your online offering.

- How many people in your organisation really understand online marketing. You may also want to find out how many of your colleagues are active on social media, whether Facebook or LinkedIn.

- Reappraise your policy on the use of social networking sites during work time. If they are currently banned, this may well prove to be the wrong course of action which won't actually improve the performance of staff.

Chapter 3

Social media has a powerful role to play in building your brand

Social media. What does it mean to you? Bored celebrities tweeting about meals they've just had at The Ivy (**www.the-ivy.co.uk**)? Drunken students posting videos they made on their phones onto YouTube? Your friends posting all their holiday photos onto Facebook and bombarding you with banal updates?

Of course, these are very commonplace activities on some of the most popular social networking sites. However, as you can see from this YouTube video by the team at Socialnomics (**www.socialnomics.net**), social media means so much more than this – **http://bit.ly/atZLs6**.

In just five years, social networking sites have emerged from nowhere to become almost ubiquitous. The newspapers are full of stories about Twitter, the police are now using Facebook to help in murder cases, kids no longer text but tweet, and YouTube videos seem to be cropping up all over the place. How has this happened and, aside from the entertainment aspect, how does this affect the way in which we do business or market ourselves?

Earlier in the book we spoke about how technological advances have dramatically transformed the way in which we communicate. A new breed of entrepreneurs – Mark Zuckerberg (Facebook), Jack Dorsey (Twitter), Jimmy Wales (Wikipedia) and a collection of former PayPal colleagues (YouTube) – used advances in software to create websites that could effectively be updated by any number of people using the minimum of technical ability.

Once you had this sort of platform, greater and greater numbers of people could then interact with the site and network online. Obviously the first adopters were the techies and the young – just watch The Social Network (**http://www.thesocialnetwork-movie.com**), the film about how Facebook started.

With digital technology came digital music, pictures and video – all our visual and aural stimulae were reduced to bytes of information which, as in the case of email, could be parcelled up and exchanged between computers.

The combination of open access websites, the easy and cheap flow of digital information, and the improvement in microprocessors meant that these new social networking sites could provide a route to an almost previously unimaginable online society.

As with virtually every other technological innovation in history, other sectors quickly cottoned onto the power of this new communications medium and quickly adapted it for their own uses – business being one of the prime movers. That is why 57% of FTSE 100 companies are now on Twitter, companies such as Starbucks have over 16 million fans on Facebook (no that's not a typo) and many organisations now have their own 'channels' on YouTube.

In fact, the development of social networking sites has prompted the move away from traditional static websites to the all singing, all dancing multimedia sites which we spoke about in the previous chapter.

Picture this: you're in a bar in Sydney with your girlfriend celebrating England winning The Ashes and you decide you want to show all your colleagues in the office in London what a great time you are having.

You can each take a video and pictures of each other using most popular smartphones. Uploading the video is very simple and it can be put onto Facebook or indeed Twitvid (**www.twitvid.com** – a video site using Twitter) within seconds, to be picked up by your friends and followers just moments later. Indeed, with the latest technology such as Facetime (**http://bit.ly/cpc8mJ**) on the iPhone 4, it is possible to broadcast yourself 'real time'.

Here's another scenario: your daughter is coming up to 18 and wants a party. Instead of sending out invites to all her friends, she simply posts an invite on Facebook along with full details of venue and what's in store for the evening. Her friends can RSVP on the site, add comments and post humorous pictures of your daughter.

During and after the party, guests can post pictures, videos and comments while your daughter can create an online album which all of her friends and family will be able to access well after the event – in fact forever!

Clearly many of you will have heard press reports talking about how these parties sometimes go horribly wrong due to hundreds of uninvited gatecrashers turning up, but it is a great example of how word of mouth is now magnified online.

If that's how individuals can now communicate with their chosen audience, think how this can be adapted for business. And that is exactly what is happening with social media. Many large organisations are now using social media intelligently as a major plank of their marketing strategies.

However, it is still seen by large parts of the business world and the older population as a fad – just another thing for people to get worked up about. And it is certainly true that sites such as Facebook, Twitter and YouTube may one day disappear, but they will just be replaced by something even more technologically advanced.

Technology is constantly evolving, new generations of people are being brought up with the likes of MySpace, Facebook and Twitter while mobile technology means these sites can pretty much be accessed anywhere. So the phenomenon is certainly not going to go away and that's why it is vitally important that you familiarise yourself with this new form of communications.

There are however four main reasons why social media is now so important for business. The important thing to remember is that using social media is absolutely **FREE** and can take very little of your time if done intelligently.

Great way to drive traffic to your website

As we explained in the previous chapter, the main goal of marketing is to drive traffic to your website and this is something social networking sites are very good at doing. In fact, they can even take the place of a website, if you simply don't have the funds available to build one.

The trick is to set up *corporate* accounts rather than personal ones. Therefore the authors have @DivadaniLtd and @2010mediauk Twitter accounts, as well as @fusionthebook – all of which are corporate accounts. However there is also @davidmiles which is used in a personal capacity, mixing the personal side with some business.

Similarly both the authors have personal Facebook pages, which are just that. However, there is also **www.facebook.com/2010media** and **www.facebook.com/divadanidesign** which are used as the business pages for our companies. In Facebook parlance these were originally known as fan pages, but are now called 'Like Pages'.

As with any good form of marketing, your corporate social media accounts can be properly branded and tailored to reflect your key messages and appeal to your key markets. Therefore, anything you upload onto these sites should be pertinent to your business, add value to your brand or can even act as short advertisements. Furthermore, when you open an account with any of the popular sites, be it Twitter, Facebook, Plaxo (**www.plaxo.com**) or Ecademy (**www.ecademy.com**), you will be asked to put in a short mission statement for your company, basic profile information, and of course your all-important website address.

In other words, just the sort of thing you would have provided to traditional directories such as Yellow Pages (now **www.yell.com**) or Thomson Local (**www.thomsonlocal.com**). The difference though is that the information is not static, can be constantly updated for free and can be far more effective at building your brand.

The key to success with social media is (a) to connect with as many people as you can (i.e. have the largest possible audience) (b) post as much fresh, interesting content as you can on your pages (have something pertinent to say) and (c) be proactive. The result will be that people read or watch your social networking sites then go to your website to find out more about your organisation or brand.

One of the most high profile examples of this in action was the Obama Presidential Campaign in 2008. Barack Obama didn't have as much financial clout as, firstly, his Democrat challengers, and then the Republican Party. He needed to reach out to as many voters as possible and educate them about his policies.

The key way of getting his message across was via his website **www.barackobama.com**.

His team realised that social networking was the way to drive people to this website and to reach the greatest possible audience for the least amount of capital outlay – fusion marketing in action. By the clever use of Twitter, YouTube and Facebook, Obama managed to reach out to millions of supporters without having to spend further limited funds on advertising campaigns (see **http://globalhumancapital.org/?p=216** for the whole story) and in so doing, ran the first major social media election campaign.

Using regular updates and drawing on the enthusiasm of his supporters, Obama managed to energise a section of the population not used to voting, or at the very least certainly not used to voting Democrat. Interestingly, a couple of years later during the UK election campaign of 2010, very few candidates had any clue about social media while some used it only intermittently (probably on the advice of their campaign managers).

One way is to get the best out of social media is to treat social networking sites as you would the traditional media. Every update should be seen as a form of press release and anything you write should be on-the-record or on message. And, as with public relations, it should contain all the information you wish to get across to your target audience(s) about your product, service or brand.

That's why it is important to understand exactly who your audience is so you can communicate your key messages succinctly.

Another way is to inject a level of personal narrative into your updates to help build 'your' brand or those of your colleagues.

Provides a clear and easy to read narrative

Building your brand online is of paramount importance, whether you are Greater Manchester Police (**http://bbc.in/cKQ8Zq**), Manchester United, Sainsbury's, a small retail business in Cornwall or a charity in Wales. Previously, organisations had to rely solely on an expensive combination of press officers, advertising and direct marketing to communicate with their audiences, stakeholders or fan base.

Now however, Twitter, YouTube and Facebook have emerged as simple, free and efficient ways to strengthen brands. No wonder that so many press offices are now switching their staff away from media relations and getting them to update social media sites instead.

Let's look again at the example of Greater Manchester Police using Twitter to log every incident it dealt with over a 24-hour period. Many papers criticised this as a waste of taxpayer's money on something they felt to be trivial but we believe it highlights just how social media can be used effectively.

In the case of the Police, their target audience for this experiment was the Government. By tweeting every call that came in, they demonstrated how busy they were and why any cuts would reduce their ability to fight crime. In effect, they strengthened the Police 'brand' in a way which would otherwise have been impossible in a pre social media era.

In a similar way, many organisations are now using Facebook pages (see **http://on.fb.me/b8k2OF** for more details) as alternatives to their websites. Bottled water producer Evian, in their recent television adverts, simply listed **www.facebook.com/evian** at the end rather than **www.evian.com** while BBC Breakfast has over 6,000 fans (or 'Likers' to give them their proper title) on their **www.facebook.com/bbcbreakfast** page.

Why do they do this when they have one of the best put-together websites in the world? There are a number of good reasons. The BBC website is enormous and can take a while to navigate so a Facebook page is much more accessible. Secondly, it can act as a trailer for programmes, thus encouraging more people to watch. Finally, it acts as a forum for discussion so that issues can be discussed in more detail while the show is off-air.

Let's take one of the hottest live bands in the world at the moment, Muse, as another example. They have their own website (**www.muse.mu**) so you may wonder why they need a Facebook page (**www.facebook.com/muse**) as well as a Twitter page and a MySpace page too.

The simple answer is that their audience (real or virtual) is unlikely to view the website every day yet many will be logging onto Facebook several times a day. Indeed, half of the 30 million Facebook accounts in the UK are accessed on a daily basis. So, with just over 7 million fans on the site, the band can market to their fan base directly without having to spend thousands on advertising.

At the other end of the scale, pressure groups such as Greenpeace (**www.facebook.com/greenpeace.international**) or Save the Children (**www.facebook.com/savethechildren**) can help raise awareness, as well as providing a forum for people all over the world to voice their concerns or express their views.

While Facebook pages are great for communicating to a predominantly consumer audience, LinkedIn can be used in very much the same way in business-to-business marketing. Groups can be set up (**http://learn.LinkedIn.com/groups/**) either in your brand name or with a title which represents what you do.

An excellent example is the Chartered Institute of Public Relations which has a group (**http://linkd.in/cyLbUE**) with over 2,600 members. This acts in much the same way as the BBC's Facebook page in that it is looking to educate those in the PR industry, it provides a forum for discussions, and acts as a corollary to the main CIPR website – **www.cipr.co.uk**.

As we said at the beginning of the book, audiences are continuing to fragment and it is getting increasingly difficult to ascertain where exactly people are going to get their information from. Therefore, by having a number of different online presences, you are tailoring your brand for the different audiences. In actual fact, this is no different from what advertisers have been doing for years in print and broadcast.

Helps improve your position on search engines

The goal of most businesses is to get their websites to the top of search engines – whether it be Google, Yahoo or Bing. There are three ways to do this. The first is through search engine optimisation (SEO), the second is through search engine marketing (e.g. Google AdWords) and the third is through regular content management of websites and social media – i.e. updating your blogs, pages, tweets, etc regularly.

One of the cheapest and easiest ways of moving towards this last goal is to be active on social media. Back in 2009, Twitter did a deal with both Google and Bing whereby tweets would be included in search results. Similarly, the more active you are on LinkedIn, the more likely it is that your name or that of your business will crop up on search engines.

That's why, with all our clients, we try to get them to link the news (or blog) feeds on their websites with their social networking sites. This way, one piece of information can go onto up to four or five different sites at the touch of a button, greatly contributing to their position on search engines.

The aim with all updates on social media, as with news updates on websites, is to include as many of your key search terms and put in as many external links to other websites as possible. In simple terms, news blogs or pages on social networking sites with the most references, will return the most relevant results and come highest on search engines.

It is also becoming standard practice to put highly visible links to your pages on social networking sites on the home page of your website.

With the 2010media website, all the company's latest tweets are automatically displayed on every page of **www.2010media.co.uk**. The result of this is that the company has shot near to the top of Google for the search term *'online PR London'*, without paying a penny in search marketing.

Can even act as a stand-alone sales tool

Social networking sites can also act as sales tools in their own right. If you build up large enough followings and post well-written and pertinent updates, you can use them as free advertisements.

Let's go back to the Starbucks example. As we said previously, they now have over 16 million fans of their Facebook page. So, every time they want to market a particular product, they have an enormous, international audience that they can effectively advertise to – **for free**.

It's hardly surprising that Facebook marketing is taking on such importance. It was recently disclosed that 1 in 12 people on the planet is on the site. Just think about it – that's a potential audience of 550 million! There are also 30 million accounts in the UK – that means half the population has an account.

In the UK alone, the vast majority of the under 30s rely on Facebook as their main source of information while even those in their 60s and 70s are using this social networking site regularly. It's an extremely powerful medium which we believe will become as ubiquitous as the mobile phone in the next couple of years.

Yet, it is still seen as somehow not being a business tool, which is a big mistake. A business Facebook page with just 25 'Likers' allows the business owner, in effect, to reserve a second branded URL for their company.

For example, the boutique hotel client in Brighton now has a well visited Facebook page **www.facebook.com/seaspraybrighton** onto which they post regular updates, pictures and videos, all for FREE. Of course, it's also possible for their customers to post positive (or negative) comments, which can either strengthen your brand or, in the case of adverse remarks, identify weaknesses in your customer service.

So successful can Facebook pages be, in fact, that for any organisation that cannot afford a website or if their website simply isn't up to the job, this can act as a very viable substitute. They can even be configured to synchronise with Twitter – helping to push your brand up search engines.

Therefore, for schools, charities, struggling retail outlets or small businesses, this may represent an ideal solution to raise their profile, in the absence of proper finances. And once there is the necessary capital, the page can simply be linked/configured with your eventual website.

Of course, if it is done in conjunction with a well optimised website, a Facebook page can act as a useful adjunct. It can not only help drive traffic to your site but you can also use it to build a network of customers to whom you can market for free.

In some cases, the Facebook page or YouTube channel for a company or organisation may actually prove to be more important than the website, so you may get the scenario where the website is there simply to build brand and drive traffic to the social networking sites.

For some larger organisations with a number of different audiences and communications channels, you may get to the stage where you have a website, Facebook page, multiple Twitter accounts and a YouTube channel. Each is there to perform a different task.

For example let's look at Channel 4 News. They have a website (**www.channel4.com/news**), a Facebook page (**www.facebook.com/Channel4News**) and the presenters each have their own (business) Twitter accounts – @channel4news, Jon Snow (@jonsnowc4), Gary Gibbon (@garygibbonblog) and Krishnan Guru-Murthy (@krishgm). They also have their own channel on YouTube (**www.youtube.com/channel4news**).

Your audience isn't in one place any more. Channel 4 News doesn't simply rely on people tuning into the programme, although this is the desired goal of ITN. Using the different forms of media, they have ensured that their brand (in this case an award-winning news and current affairs programme), is seen by the widest number of people.

Another example is the UK's largest retailer, Tesco, with hundreds of thousands of different product lines, a myriad of audiences and a multitude of messages to get across.

Their website **www.tesco.com** is the first port of call for people wishing to find out about the company, its stores and products. However, they also have numerous Facebook pages – e.g. **www.facebook.com/clothingattesco**,

www.facebook.com/tescogreenerliving – and a multitude of Twitter accounts: @tescostores, @tescocareers, @clothingattesco, @tescomobile and @tescofootball.

In fact, recently the company launched a major study looking into the effectiveness of Twitter as a way of engaging with its customers. The head of research and development at Tesco.com was quoted as saying that they were looking to engage with customers through sites like Twitter. See (**http://bit.ly/eKhHrm**) for more details.

A word of warning though. While it is easy for you to build your brand on social media, using sites like Facebook and Twitter, so it is for your disgruntled customers or those with an axe to grind to harm your brand. For this reason, some organisations are preferring to have no presence on social networking sites so as to prevent people writing unwanted comments. There will be more on this in Chapter 11 where we'll look at why this is the wrong stance to take.

This is an important issue and it cuts across not just PR and marketing, but also customer relations. Before setting up accounts, then, it is imperative that there is buy-in from your team and you have a joined-up policy among your different departments.

However, even this negative can be made into a positive. Traditionally, people would complain publicly – generally by writing to or calling up newspapers – if the communication channels were closed. Now there are many different ways of communicating with an organisation, so it is easier to nip problems in the bud before they get too serious. Similarly, if there are many people complaining via Facebook or Twitter, you clearly have a problem that needs to be dealt with rather than hidden under the carpet.

One example is South Eastern Trains. During a recent spate of bad weather, the service they provided was less than adequate and, as many commuters are armed with smartphones, people made their complaints vocally on Twitter. Indeed some commuters went a stage further and set up their own Twitter account – **www.twitter.com/_southeastern** to have a go at the standard of the service they received.

Other ways in which social media can assist your business

Along with the four key reasons mentioned earlier, there are a number of other ways in which social media can leverage your business:

Promotion and sales

Computer giant Dell recently made its first million dollars via Twitter. People who have signed up to follow the company receive messages or tweets when discounted products are available at the company's Dell Home Outlet Store. Dell started to experiment with Twitter in March 2007 and there are now 65 Dell accounts or Dell Twitter Groups on Twitter.

Customer service

When monitoring social media on a regular basis, organisations can gauge what their customers think about them and act accordingly. The most high profile example of this is Trip Advisor where hotels are ranked online by guests. Hotels then have to make sure their service is up to scratch.

Building brand loyalty

By having large numbers of followers and fans on social media, you are creating exclusive networks of people you can market to for free. Footwear giant Nike has nearly 4 million fans on Facebook and, as a result, has been able to cut back on traditional advertising.

Monitoring the competition

As we are now living in a much more open society with large amounts of information visible online, it is possible to see what your competitors are doing by monitoring their social media sites. Of course they can see yours too. That's why it is important to stress the characters and personalities of your staff as well as your brand.

Online networking

Twitter and LinkedIn are great ways of networking without having to leave your PC or, as is now the case, your phone. Simply post what product or service you are on the look-out for and, as long as you have built up a decent sized network, you will usually get some form of referral or business lead.

LinkedIn is also a versatile tool to find people within specific companies and professions. Many people on the site have 500+ connections, which means they start to become very useful people to know. Furthermore, by accessing forums on the site, it is possible to communicate with the people in your target markets.

Customer feedback

Testimonials are always of paramount importance in business. Both LinkedIn and Facebook have the facility for people to give you feedback on your personal level of service (LinkedIn) or your company's service (Facebook).

It must be said that in the case of Facebook (or, as previously mentioned, TripAdvisor) the feedback can be negative. In this case, it helps you to correct any mistakes that have been made so you can provide a better service in the future.

Suggested action plan

- Find out how many of your friends, clients, colleagues and families are on social networking sites and ascertain how regularly they access their accounts.

- If you don't have an account, ask a friend or colleague to show you around the key social networking sites. At the same time, even if you are not signed up to any of the accounts, you will still be able to view individual pages – just click on any of the links within this chapter.

- Monitor what your competitors are doing. If they have social media accounts and are using them successfully, they will be stealing a march on you, as well as stealing potential customers.

- Do NOT sign up to any social media accounts until you know what it is you wish to say and exactly who your target audience is – we shall be coming onto this later. Of course, in the meantime, there is no harm in setting up personal accounts and this could be a useful way of starting to get an understanding of how social media works.

- If you do have access to social media, look up your favourite brands to see how they use the sites to leverage their brand.

Chapter 4

Reach a potentially unlimited audience for no extra cost

Social media, then, gives you the tools to communicate, but how best to use them? Like with any other form of networking, it pays to be as proactive as possible and have something pertinent to say – just as if you were walking into a room full of potential clients or introducers.

Imagine you are on a stage in a business venue with nine of your closest competitors. This is not unlike the virtual situation which exists on the first page of search engines. Most people searching for something on Google will never get past the first page of search results – the top ten.

Sitting in front of you are a hundred of your ideal clients or key stakeholders. They are eagerly trying to establish what it is that differentiates you from the other people on the stage.

Your job is to put on a 'show' which reflects your personality and brand, and pushes enough of your unique selling points (USPs). If done successfully enough, your audience will warm to you more than your competitors and want to buy your product or service. At the same time, they may leave the building and tell their friends, loved ones and colleagues about you.

The same is true online. Your direct audience are the people who come directly to your website or find you by searching on Google, Yahoo or Bing. Social networking sites are the way in which your product, service or brand is spread through word of mouth.

The key thing is to make sure your audience is constantly growing and you are continually refining your messages to keep your target markets interested in what you have to say. That way you give yourself as much chance as possible to win new business. At the same time, it will help to ensure that your competitors don't gain a business advantage over you.

Regularly update blogs and social media sites

Like with any form of networking, the more you put into online marketing, the more you will get out. Many people in business get excited about the possibilities of setting up news pages on their websites or corporate social media accounts, then are disappointed when they don't get a quick return.

It is not unsurprising, then, that according to recent figures, 80% of Twitter accounts are actually inactive (**http://bit.ly/cfegfY**). At the same time, how often have you visited a website's news page to find it hasn't been updated for months?

With online marketing and social media you are, metaphorically speaking, entering a vast room full of an almost infinite number of organisations and individuals – a fantasy trade fair if you like. Therefore, to make the most out of this opportunity you MUST:

(a) have something to say
(b) have an idea about the sort of people you wish to meet and
(c) try and seek out as many of these people as possible.

If you do, you will more than likely initiate conversations with target clients or customers. But don't, as the above Twitter statistic suggests many people are doing, go into the 'room' and assume that lots of people are going to come up to you suddenly and start wanting to do business with you. This simply will not happen.

So, the first stage in making your presence or brand felt online is to set up a blog or dedicated news page on your website. Depending on your budget, this can be done in a number of different ways:

- If you have no website, use your Facebook page (see Chapter 3) as a news feed.

- If your existing website is fairly up-to-date, then you can incorporate a blog into the site using easy-to-use software such as Wordpress (**www.wordpress.org**). This would need to be done by a web designer but can cost as little as £400.

- If your website is over three years old or cannot be altered, you may want to think about investing in a new site with a built-in news feed using Wordpress or other platforms such as Drupal (**www.drupal.org**) or Joomla (**www.joomla.org**).

All of the above can be integrated with other social media platforms. For example, Facebook can be easily configured to 'feed' Twitter automatically, Wordpress can be set up to update both Twitter and Facebook, while Twitter can update LinkedIn (or vice versa).

There is even a site called Ping (**www.ping.fm**) which can be used to update a huge range of social networks simultaneously, thus negating the argument "I haven't got time to update all my different sites".

Whatever set-up you choose, the next step is to make sure you update the blog on a regular basis. This can vary, according to the industry or profession you are in, but at the very least it should be once a week or ideally once a day.

This news page should have updates on anything pertinent to you, your staff, your industry sector or your target markets – in effect, it should almost act like an online newsletter. Where possible there should be hyperlinks to salient press articles, websites or other blogs and it should also be used as a way to advertise other pages on your website via internal links – thereby increasing traffic across the pages of your website.

Remember, your website is your shop window. Like any good department store, this shop window should be changed frequently to maintain interest and reflect your target markets' desires.

It is hardly surprising, then, that many larger organisations with in-house press offices are starting to employ people in social media relations while many PR agencies have now renamed themselves as Integrated Social Media & PR agencies.

As with public relations, though, it is vital that you understand your audience and communicate with them in a way they will understand. And whatever you do, make sure you write in an easy-to-read way – think tabloid style rather than old-fashioned broadsheet.

Building up networks of followers

Now you have something to say, you want to have an audience. With social media, you have the answer. Facebook has over 550 million people registered on the site (as of January 2011), Twitter has over 200 million users (as of February 2011) while LinkedIn has over 100 million members (as of March 2011). At the same time, YouTube is now one of the three most visited websites in the world and the second most visited search engine after Google.

That's an enormous group of people to communicate with, but how do you begin to tap into these vast networks and how can you make sure your messages are being correctly received? Let's look at three key social media sites in turn to see how this can be done. All are free to set up and use, they take very little time and all have their own apps (see **http://bit.ly/bVG5Pb**) so they can be used on the move with iPhones, Blackberries or other smartphones.

Twitter – www.twitter.com

This 'micro-blogging' site is the perfect way to get short messages across to large numbers of people and is therefore an incredibly powerful and cost-effective brand-building tool. Not only can it be set up to mirror the look and feel of your website but it also publicises your mission statement – the one-line sentence which sums up who you are and what you do.

In essence, Twitter is a way of publicising yourself or your product in 140 character updates. This may not seem very much, but used cleverly, you can convey large amounts of information to help build your brand.

It acts as a news feed, with 'tweets' being updated almost every second. Once you are logged in, every time you go onto Twitter – or in fact a host of Twitter platforms such as Tweetdeck (**www.tweetdeck.com**) or Hootsuite (**www.hootsuite.com**) – you will get a real-time feed of updates from the people and organisations you are following.

The more accounts you choose to follow, the more updates you will get. Therefore if you were only following the tweets of ten people who weren't very prolific at updating, your feed would be pretty empty. Conversely, if you're following 2,000 people, you'll be getting a steady stream of information – hence the reason some press officers are now social media relations officers so they can monitor these updates.

And if you are worried about information overload, you can always create a folder with all your favourite people/ organisations. You can also build category lists. For example **www.twitter.com/2010mediauk/hotels** contains a list of all the hotel/hospitality people 2010media follows.

While setting up an account can take less than five minutes, building up a network of followers can take a while, depending on how active you choose to be. Therefore, the real investment is the time dedicated to building a following as well as uploading updates.

As previously stated, your Twitter page can be fed automatically from your blog. Or there is no reason why you cannot update it separately or even via your LinkedIn account.

Therefore, if you are, say, a recruitment consultant or estate agent, you could advertise jobs or properties via your page. Similarly, if you simply need to get a message out to a large number of people, Twitter is a great way to do it.

In fact, Twitter has become so successful that it is now starting to replace both email and text messaging. Why? Because it is a fast way to communicate with multiple people, it can be used on all but the most basic phones, you can squeeze large amounts of data into just 140 characters – including pictures, videos or downloads – and it is free.

For example, well-known high street brand Marks & Spencer (**www.twitter.com/marksandspencer**) has almost 16,000 followers. They use Twitter for a variety of uses from advertising product lines to dealing with customer service issues and talking about issues pertaining to their business.

The trick with Twitter is to follow as many people as possible who are pertinent to your target audience(s). In other words, you would want to follow companies you could do business *for*, as well as organisations you could do business in partnership *with*.

If you are following the right organisations, a high proportion of these Twitter users will follow you back, see your mission statement and hopefully go to your website. You will then also be able to message them directly – potentially creating a valuable business relationship.

LinkedIn – www.linkedin.com

Originally set up as a recruitment site in 2003, LinkedIn has now grown enormously to become the Facebook of the business world. At its most basic, if you create a profile on the site, it becomes your online CV listing your work experience, education and recommendations. However, used properly, it can again be a powerful way to leverage your brand.

As with all social media sites, it takes very little time to open an account with LinkedIn. Just fill in your basic details, the mission statement for your company, website address and, of course, add a well-taken photograph of yourself. If applicable, all your staff should also be encouraged to create accounts too. This helps to build their personal brands as well as reinforcing your corporate brand.

While it takes just a few minutes to create a profile, to market yourself in the best light, you need to make sure your profile is 100% complete. Therefore details of your education, qualifications, past employers, experience and even interests should be filled in.

Also, one of the most important elements of LinkedIn is the ability to give and receive recommendations, a vital way to boost your own profile or the profiles of the people you work for/with. All of your recommendations can then be used on your website as testimonials.

Once you have a profile you are proud of, the next step is to connect with as many people as you can on the site. This can be done in a number of ways. The easiest is to use the LinkedIn/

Outlook toolbar (**http://linkd.in/a96u3A**). This will go through all the contacts you have in Microsoft Outlook, tell you which are on LinkedIn and then invite you to connect with them automatically. Not only that, but it also provides a dashboard which keeps you up-to-date with your connections.

The second way to connect is to make sure that whenever you meet anyone new (be it through networking, business meetings or otherwise), as soon as you get their business card or contact details, make sure you invite them to connect with you. This is now an accepted way of staying in touch with business contacts.

Finally, you can look up people or companies on the site via the search function. If they are people you know directly, then you can send them a message via the site, asking them to connect. You can also ask to connect to someone you don't know, but only if you have a mutual contact who can act as an introducer.

Once you've built up a network of contacts, as with Twitter, you want to start communicating with this audience. The simplest way is to update the Network Activity box on the home page, once you've signed in. This is exactly the same size as the box on Twitter (140 characters) and can also be configured to update a Twitter page automatically.

As with Facebook, you can also create group and business profiles on LinkedIn to help raise the profile of your brand or organisation even further. Invite your customers, clients and business partners to join these groups so you can create an effective way of communicating your key messages on a regular basis. This will provide you with another chance to publicise your mission statement and key messages. You can also post news on it, as you would on your blog or Facebook page.

At the same time, there are also thousands of groups you can join on LinkedIn. Simply type a topic into the search bar and it will come up with the relevant groups. You can request to join any group you wish and, if accepted by the administrator, start communicating with other members. It is similar to the notion of powerteams in business networking, where people in similar or related businesses team up for mutual benefit.

Facebook – www.facebook.com

Over 550 million people in the world now have Facebook accounts with over 30 million in the UK. That makes it a very powerful marketing tool.

We've already spoken about how a Facebook page can effectively double as a second website for your organisation or brand. However, as with every form of marketing, you need to access the right audience and this is a little more time intensive than it is with Twitter.

The key target you need to aim for is to get 25 people to 'Like' your page. Once you have achieved this goal you can log onto Facebook (**www.facebook.com/username**), reserve the name you wish and, hey presto, you've got a second website you can use for marketing.

With using Facebook on a personal level, the idea is to connect to as many people who know, so you can 'socialise' with them online. To find your friends, you can use the friend finder or look for them via the search function.

It is different with your business page. Here, you are trying to get as many people as possible to show that they are a fan of your business by clicking the 'Like' button on your Facebook page. As with a new website, no one will know it's there though so you need to start building a fan base.

The free way to do this is through word of mouth, via a link on your website, email signatures or through traditional printed marketing materials. You may even prefer to use your Facebook page in marketing rather than your website, depending on your target audience.

For example, the Afton Hotel caters for two very different markets – coach parties of elderly people, as well as people from the local Eastbourne area who are interested in a live music venue or somewhere to hold weddings.

With the first group, it would be sensible to use **www.aftonhotel.co.uk** on any printed literature, because for people in this age group this will be the main way of learning about the hotel online. Remember, the fastest growing sector of people accessing the internet is the 50- and 60-somethings so the website needs to be up to the job.

However, it may be that the hotel's Facebook page is a much better advertising medium for them to use to access the local market. Many of the target audience will be younger and have Facebook accounts which they access daily at home and via their mobiles. They will therefore be more likely to bookmark **www.facebook.com/aftonhotel** instead of the hotel's own website.

Of course there is another alternative, which involves spending money (although not very much) and which can be very cost effective, particularly if you are marketing directly to consumers. This is pay-per-click Facebook advertising and is used in exactly the same way as in search engine marketing. As with Google AdWords, the adverts are on the right hand side of the Facebook page (**www.facebook.com/advertising**).

The difference here is that with over 30 million UK accounts and the huge amount of data kept on people, it is possible to segment your target audience far more accurately than if you were using traditional advertising.

Therefore, if you wanted to sell t-shirts to girls aged 16-20, who live in the Midlands, like bands such as Lostprophets (**www.facebook.com/lostprophets**) & Funeral for a Friend (**www.facebook.com/funeralforafriend**), enjoy eating KFC (**www.facebook.com/KFC**) and are fans of the TV programme Misfits (**www.facebook.com/e4misfits**), Facebook will come up with a number of people who match this criteria. Then, each time they log into their account, they will see the t-shirt ads. You can even get analytics for the number of page impressions and clicks that the ad generates.

YouTube – www.youtube.com

YouTube is now the second most used search engine after Google with two billion (yes, that's right) views per day (**http://bit.ly/hpLhqy**). This also makes it one of the most visited websites in the world and a great place to leverage your brand.

The ability to take high quality video has never been easier – think back twenty years to the old bulky video cameras then look at the iPhones and Android phones of today. Moving images are increasingly seen as the norm on websites as well as on the other social media sites.

In the same way as with Facebook, organisations can open both their own branded accounts and 'channel' on YouTube. This means they get to reserve their own YouTube URL. For example **www.youtube.com/blur** or **www.youtube.com/xfactor** will take you straight through to the videos and information for these two brands.

The pages will also act as yet another way to publicise your key messages, reach your target markets and help drive traffic to your website.

The key thing here is that once you have uploaded a video to YouTube, you're effectively giving the clip its own URL which can then be posted on blogs, tweeted (or you can upload them straight to **www.twitpic.com**), embedded into your website, or emailed.

Of course, having a presence on such a well-used website as YouTube will also help improve your search rankings, thereby further leveraging your brand.

Think about the possibilities of having your own video channel. Take for example what could be done in the hospitality industry. Hotels would be able to show guests around before they book, restaurants could show prospective diners how the chef prepares the food, leisure attractions could shoot client testimonials.

A good example of how this can be done is Best Western Hotels Great Britain (**www.youtube.com/bestwesterngb**). This hotel chain uses its channel on YouTube to publicise some of its staff and give the brand a human, more personal side.

Similarly, estate agents can use video to show clients 'virtually' around houses, to promote the areas in which properties are situated or, again, to give individual sales consultants the chance to sell themselves – something done successfully by Frank Harris (**www.youtube.com/frankharris81**) on YouTube and also on their website (**www.frankharris.co.uk**).

Clearly, the cost of putting together a promotional film can sometimes be prohibitive, but there is even a way around this using a collaborative approach. Let's take hotels as an example again – this time at the smaller, boutique end of the industry. Like any hotel, the Sea Spray hotel in Brighton works with a large number of suppliers and has contact with a myriad number of organisations in the town such as taxi firms, bars, restaurants and places of interest.

Any guest, when staying at the hotel, has access to these companies via an excellent menu of services that the management provides. However, prior to checking in, potential or future guests have little idea of what is on offer. Therefore the hotel has teamed up with a number of its affiliate partners to produce a promotional video.

This way, everyone benefits and the cost is shared out between the companies represented in the film – each of whom will be able to take the YouTube URL to publicise themselves online too via their own websites or social media pages.

Whether you use a video production company or simply the video function on your smartphone, the use of moving images is a powerful sales tool which can do so much more for your brand than any traditional marketing.

Suggested action plan

- See whether there is anyone within your organisation who may be willing or able to write a blog/news page on your website. Also see if they would have the time to spend on building up a following on sites such as Twitter.

- Speak to your existing web designer to see how much it would cost to get a blog embedded into your website. This really shouldn't be expensive - in most cases no more than around £400 or £500.

- If you don't already have an account, sign up to LinkedIn and try to encourage all your colleagues to do so too. Even better, add your LinkedIn profiles to your email signature and to the About Us section of your website.

- Look at the main social networking sites and see how applicable they could be to your business.

- See whether there are any potential affiliate partners who would be willing to contribute to the cost of a video aimed at social media.

Chapter 5

Reduce spending on out-of-date marketing activities

It's clear that we are now in an era of change. Many of the underlying assumptions about how we market to our target audiences have been turned on their head by the online revolution. There is still a huge resistance on the part of many business owners and marketing managers to change, and a reluctance to alter standard working practices that have barely been updated since the 1980s or even further back than that.

Let's take as an example the property industry. With the growth in private development firms building houses in the 1980s on the back of the property boom of that decade, the model for property marketing was created: produce a high quality brochure, spend money on a sales suite and/or show home, place a series of ads in the press and secure the services of a PR agency.

Until the last couple of years, this model worked fine. The advertising would bring in scores of interested buyers, the PR would build the brand of the development and add further demand before the brochures were then sent out or given to potential purchasers as they toured the scheme.

The main idea was to get people phoning up. And this is key. The younger generation simply don't like picking up the phone and would rather get all their information online. Even 30 and 40-somethings prefer to do due diligence and background research before lifting the phone to call someone in the sales suite.

Yet still there are dozens of property developers, housebuilders and housing associations who continue with this model despite the changing media consumption habits of their target audiences.

As we pointed out earlier, though, some of these traditional marketing tools still work. Many developments need a certain number of brochures, a level of targeted advertising can be useful to drive sales to a website, while the public relations has its place in creating an awareness about the brand and supports the sales effort.

The key to success is understanding how exactly your target audiences consume the media and matching your marketing investment accordingly. It is vital to test and measure each pound you are spending to ensure you are getting the maximum possible return.

Be brave!

There is a saying that 'fortune favours the brave' and this is particularly true when formulating a new marketing strategy. Stopping what you have traditionally done for decades can be a daunting prospect for many business owners and there is a real fear of the unknown. As it was at the start of the internet era in the mid to late 1990s with the first introduction of websites, there is the feeling that much modern marketing is merely a fad and that old-style approaches still work. As a result, many business owners are loathe to change their habits.

That's why so many companies continue to spend vast sums of money on printed materials such as brochures, newsletters and even in-house magazines. At the same time, many managing directors and even marketing managers would consider it foolhardy to stop spending money on advertising and public relations.

Yet by tracking the return on investment (ROI) in detail of all these marketing tools, it may become evident that a lot of money is simply being poured down the drain and that there may need to be a change in emphasis on where the marketing investment is targeted.

The great thing about online marketing is that much of it is free. Therefore, you can run it in tandem with your traditional marketing to see what difference it makes to your level of sales and, ultimately, your profits.

Let's take a local pub as an example. Many of the customers are regulars, the target audience may live within walking distance and its offering is fairly basic – drink and food. One would think that listings in local publications, directories such as Yellow Pages or Thomson, plus some fliers would probably do the trick.

Yet even here, the business could benefit from some simple online marketing tools which would prove more effective. Using a

Facebook page, the pub could use the power of its loyal customer base to extol the virtues of the establishment, it could advertise special events and even offer discounts to Facebook fans. Using Google AdWords they could hit a specially-selected audience of people who are drawn to the area the pub serves as well as publicising key events such as Christmas, Easter, Mothers' Day, etc.

An excellent example of this is Renaissance Pubs (**www.renaissancepubs.co.uk**) who are successfully using their Facebook page (**www.facebook.com/renaissancepubs**) to build their online brand.

If you choose not to try out different forms of marketing then the consequences could be terminal. There are large numbers of businesses that still have no web presence or one that is not up to the job. Instead, many of them will just keep doing what they've always done, with ever decreasing returns, until their business folds. At a time when marketing budgets are being stretched to the limit and banks are refusing to extend lines of credit to businesses, it doesn't make sense to carry on doing what you've always done.

So for those people who are still sceptical about online marketing and need hard evidence before they can change their mindset, there are some simple steps that can be taken which will provide them with the data they need to reappraise the way they market themselves.

The simplest way is to look at your sales figures. Year-on-year, allowing for the economic downturn or other external factors such as extreme weather events, are they decreasing, staying the same, or increasing? If sales are static or dropping, in many cases, it will be the marketing that is at fault. Yet we would argue that even if the sales figures are healthy, it is always worth keeping one eye on the future in case your target audiences change how they wish to consume the media.

A good illustration of this is nursing homes. Clearly designed for the older generation, the marketing will be based around potential customers or their middle aged children. Therefore, a well designed brochure plus a simple website may suffice for now. However, fast-forward a few years: many of the target audience will be far more tech-savvy and will have a greater thirst for online information. Therefore those nursing homes with social media links, video testimonials on YouTube, a news page which is updated daily and detailed biographies of key staff will attract customers more readily than those which stick to current marketing methods.

Another easy way to get a perspective on your marketing is to ask your staff what they think and let them tell you if there are customer bases they think you should be reaching but which you currently are not. Younger members of your team may spot openings or new audiences that you had previously overlooked – so listen to them.

One thing is certain, with the fragmentation of the media, it is almost impossible to say with certainty exactly how people are going to find out about your product or service. Therefore there has to be a constant reappraisal of who your target audience is and how you can reach them.

Thinking about your target audience(s)

Many people running commercial operations think they know exactly who their customers are. If they did not, they probably wouldn't (or shouldn't) be in business. Local shops know most of their trade will come from within a ten mile radius. Professional services firms such as lawyers or accountants would look for people seeking their specialised skill sets. Indian restaurants cater for people who like spicy food from the Indian sub-continent.

It is therefore imperative that your marketing is tailored exactly for these target markets. At the same time, business owners need to think about emerging markets and how to access these effectively.

A useful exercise would be to sit down with colleagues or your business advisor and draw up a list of your key customers. Who are they, how do you communicate with them, how could you market to them more effectively and how are their needs likely to change over the coming years?

Then look at your business and, given that 99% of us wish to grow commercially, see where you could attract more customers. Are you running an hotel where you would like to build up the events and weddings side of the business? Are you a restaurant that wants to capitalise on the lunchtime business market? Are you an organic greengrocer who wants to tempt customers away from Waitrose?

With all these examples, it is important that you spend time looking at these markets – current or potential – understand who they are, establish the best way to market to them and which types of media will work best. It may be worth putting together a questionnaire for your current clients/customers, asking them what forms of advertising or marketing most attract them.

When segmenting your audience, age becomes one of the most important factors. As we've already mentioned, members of Generation Y do not behave in the same way when it comes to media consumption as their parents or even elder siblings' generations. The younger your target audience, the less likely that traditional marketing will work and the more likely you are to be wasting your money.

Therefore, if you are an independent retailer trying to market to people aged between 18 and 25, although advertising may still work for you, it may prove too costly. Better to save your money and reallocate it onto your website as well as perhaps a Google Adwords and Facebook pay-per-click campaign.

If you do decide to go down the route of putting together a questionnaire, it should be repeated on an annual basis to see how people's habits are changing. Remember our earlier comments about the year-on-year decline in newspaper circulations and the rise in the number of people on social media. As a result, there is an ever-changing shift in media consumption. With increased access to wifi networks, the appearance of tablets (like the iPad) and continued investment in 3G and 4G technology, we will become more of a wireless society and steadily less reliant on paper-based marketing.

So it is highly likely your client base will also be changing how they access the media. A good example of this is Coca-Cola. Traditionally Coca-Cola will have spent millions of dollars on multi-level, international advertising campaigns. However, as early adopters of social media, they quickly built up a fan base on their Facebook page and now have over 22 million people to market to for free. As a result, far less money will now be spent on advertising.

At the smaller end of the scale, many estate agents produce quarterly glossy magazines to promote themselves, the services they offer and the properties they are selling or renting. These magazines served an important purpose during the 80s and 90s as people expected more from the property industry. However, these magazines cost thousands of pounds to produce and distribute, yet have a shelf life of just a few weeks. Is this really a sensible use of marketing spend?

Google Analytics – the window on your window on the world!

For anyone with a website though – and if you don't have one, get one (!) – the single best way to ascertain exactly how your marketing is performing is via Google Analytics (**www.google.com/analytics**).

This free piece of software can be embedded in almost any website to provide you with an incredibly detailed report showing exactly how your site is performing.... or not, as the case may be. Data such as number of visits, geographical spread of visitors, most visited pages, keyword searches on search engines and traffic sources can all be found at the touch of a button.

Not only does this allow you to make key decisions about whether to upgrade/replace your website but it also helps you track the effectiveness of all the other marketing tools at your disposal. It is so sophisticated that it can tell you how many people viewed your site on mobile devices – even what make they viewed it on, be it iPhone, Blackberry, etc.

Most importantly, though, it may save you large amounts of money you would otherwise have wasted on marketing that is no longer applicable or effective. How? By illustrating both the amount of traffic and the quality of traffic being driven to your website.

Going back to our example of the estate agents producing in-house glossy magazines which they then send out to a large mailing list of clients and prospective clients, a quick look at their analytics in the weeks after publication would give them an easy overview of how successful it had been in driving traffic to their website – there should be some form of spike in traffic numbers. In fact, it would even be possible to find out which pages visitors to the website had then clicked on – thereby giving an accurate report into the effectiveness of this piece of marketing.

Similarly, if you were a restaurant and had spent money on a direct mail campaign, sending fliers out to a wide number of postcodes, you would quickly see how many people had then decided to look at your website.

A good case study of this in practice is the specialist granite worktop company Granite Transformations (**www.granitetransformations.co.uk**). They use a wide range of traditional and online marketing tools to help sell their products.

In addition to having a highly optimised website plus social media presence, they also advertise in a range of lifestyle publications, as well as using a specialist PR consultant. By monitoring the analytics on a regular basis, they can clearly see how much traffic has been driven to their website from the online versions of the publications they have appeared in and can use this to understand how many of these leads turn into sales.

Should there be no, or very few, leads from any of these publications (whether generated from advertising or public relations), then they can stop using them immediately, thereby freeing up marketing investment to spend on tools that do work.

The statistics do need to be monitored on a regular basis, though, to establish how well your site is performing and also find out exactly who/what your online audience is. Many companies have analytics on their site and have never bothered to check it or simply don't know what to do with the data.

If you don't already have it, it is very simple to set up analytics on your website. You go to **www.google.com/analytics**, follow the instructions and open your (free) account. You'll then be given some code which will need to be embedded into each of the pages on your website. This should be something that your web designer will be able to do for either a small fee or even gratis if you ask them nicely!

Once it is on your site, you will be able to log-in and monitor how your site is performing whenever you wish – even hourly if you are running a campaign and want to see how it is progressing real time. Alternatively, you can set it up to send you through a report automatically once a week/fortnight/month – as you wish. These reports can be saved as a PDF or Excel spreadsheet to make it easy for you to send to colleagues, business partners, etc.

Once the analytics is up and running, you must set up a number of key performance indicators (KPIs) so you can measure the following:

1. Number of visitors to your website – this is measured as new visitors or repeat visitors. From this you can ascertain how many people over a delineated time period came to your site.
2. Bounce rate – the percentage of visits in which the person left your site without progressing beyond the first page. Generally speaking, the lower this is, the better – anything between 30% and 60% is acceptable.
3. Time spent on site – clearly if people are spending very little time on your site it is a problem. For most websites with four or more pages and a proper level of content you would hope to see something in excess of two minutes.
4. Time spent on specific pages – you will know the importance of the various pages which make up your website. If people are spending very little time on these pages, you may want to think about making them more appealing or search friendly.
5. Most visited pages – clearly some pages will be more interesting to visitors than others. The bulk of people will go

to your home page followed by the about us and contact us pages. As with the time spent on specific pages, if some pages are getting little traffic it is probably because they aren't of interest or are difficult to find.

6. Traffic sources – people can come to your website from a wide variety of different sources. Some large companies will have traffic sources in the thousands. The most common, though, will be search engines such as Google, direct (i.e. typing your address into the browser), web portals (e.g. **www.primelocation.com**, **www.lastminute.com**, **www.laterooms.com**), online publications (**www.telegraph.co.uk**) and social media.

7. Search terms used in search engines – this will tell you what people have typed into Google, Bing or Yahoo to get to your website. This is important as it plays a vital role in search engine optimisation and also in any pay-per-click campaign you may decide to undertake.

8. Geographic spread of visitors – depending on the nature of your business, you will know the geographical location of your target audience. Therefore this should be reflected in the statistics. If you are business based in Newcastle but are selling to people nationally, then if only a minority of visits to the website are from outside the North East, clearly there is an issue with your marketing.

9. Visitors via mobile internet – more and more people now access the internet on mobile browsers. While the figures are low (around 5% for most websites) they are growing almost exponentially and will make up a sizeable proportion of visitors within the next two or three years.

Over time, you will then be able to build up an in-depth understanding of your current customer base as well as identifying the markets you are currently not able to penetrate. However, you can **only** track how your site is performing once you have analytics embedded – it cannot be done retrospectively. That's why you need to get it onto your site at once.

The advantage of having had analytics on your site for one or more years is that you can start comparing like with like. Clearly, as a retailer, there is no point comparing December with August as they are wholly different sales periods. Whereas if you were able to compare December 2010 with December 2009 and December 2008, you would be able to get an accurate picture about your performance during the key pre-Christmas sales period.

For those companies who want to get an even more complete picture about how their websites are performing, there are other software packages you can buy which give even more in-depth information about visitors to your site – from tracking mouse movements on individual pages to further data about the geographical location of visitors.

Furthermore, if you are mounting a campaign in a number of different publications, using unique landing pages (a single web page that someone is directed to by a particular advertisement), you can even track how much traffic was driven by each individual advert. Thus, you can ascertain what return on investment (ROI) you are getting from each advert.

And if you decide to begin a Google AdWords (pay-per-click) campaign to help advertise one of your products or services (something we will discuss in more detail in a later chapter), again the analytics on your website, along with the reports you get from Google, will provide an accurate assessment of how your strategy is faring. As well as illustrating how many people visit your site from Google organically (i.e. typing in keywords to Google and arriving at your site after seeing you listed in the natural/organic results), it will also indicate how many people are visiting the site as a result of clicking on your sponsored link in the Google AdWords results.

Whether you use Google Analytics or an alternative, paid-for, software product, you will quickly build up an exact picture of how the world views your brand, via your website. It is therefore important that you get to grips with the key performance indicators and you regularly monitor these, as you would any business goals for your company.

If this is something that you do not feel comfortable doing, you may want to allocate this role to someone else in the company or work with an outside marketing specialist who will be able to interpret the data for you and send you easy-to-understand reports which highlight the KPIs and enable you to focus on any areas which are weak.

Testing and measuring

With any kind of advertising or marketing, you've got to test different ideas and measure the results in order to know whether what you are doing has given you an improvement and whether it was worth whatever time or money you invested in order to put the idea into practice.

For example, an online advertising campaign that costs you £1,000 might seem expensive, but if you can prove that it brought you three new clients who each spent £3,000 then suddenly it seems pretty reasonable. By the same token, a seemingly cheap £50 classified advert in a local paper is actually very expensive if it brings you no new business whatsoever. It's only once you test and measure that you can decide if a particular marketing idea (online or offline) was a wise move or not.

One of the beauties of online marketing is that it is pretty easy to make regular and rapid changes to your website itself or to your online advertising campaigns (e.g. Google AdWords). So if you have a new idea that you want to test, you can try it out quickly.

But to do this effectively you need to focus on one change or idea at a time – because that's the only way you can say for certain which of your various ideas to improve your website end up being the one(s) which actually make a difference.

That's why people who are serious about increasing the effectiveness of their internet marketing have to take things a bit slower and not try to do everything overnight. And that's why, if you're working with a web designer, an SEO specialist, or an AdWords consultant, you need to find someone you can work with long term and who can be available to help you monitor your results and make further recommendations and changes on an ongoing basis.

Not every idea that you implement to try to get more enquiries from your website will work, but by testing and measuring effectively you can quickly abandon the things which don't bring any improvements, and focus on doing more of the same in the case of those that are proven to make a positive difference.

Suggested action plan

- Get Google Analytics embedded into your website straight away and familiarise yourself with what it can do. If you already have analytics, make sure you look at it at least once a week and, where possible, review your website's current performance against previous months or years.

- If there is no one in your company who can understand/ interpret the analytics, work with an outside marketing consultant on a monthly retainer.

- Establish some key performance indicators for your website so you can set goals for your business.

- Establish who exactly your key markets are and match your marketing to them.

- Through analytics, measure the ROI from your current marketing and if needs be, ditch or alter anything that does not drive sales or traffic to your website.

- Test and measure on a regular and on-going basis.

- Question your target customers/clients about what marketing works best for them and build your strategy around this.

- Regularly question these key audiences to see if their media consumption habits have changed.

Chapter 6
Define who you are as an organisation

In the last chapter we looked at carefully defining who exactly your target audience is. Now it's time to look in the mirror and have a good look at yourself and your organisation. This is of paramount importance as it will influence everything you do from face-to-face networking to online marketing, PR and social media.

At a typical networking group that meets on a weekly or fortnightly basis, attendees usually have to stand up and give a 60 second presentation on themselves, their company and the type of business they are looking for that week. Put yourselves in their shoes for a minute. If you were asked to give a one minute presentation to a group of business people, would you be able to communicate what it is you do and the sort of markets you are aiming to access?

The great thing about networking regularly is that you will soon find out if your messages are getting across. Either people will not really understand what it is you do, or they will and you'll begin to get new business leads. Every week you're under the spotlight, testing the quality of your presentation skills and measuring how well you are conveying your key messages. It is quickly evident from some of the presentations that you'll see at a typical networking meeting that some people aren't entirely sure what their key messages are.

In the same way, a quick glance at many business websites reveals very little about what that company does. How many times have you gone onto a home page and had very little clue about the nature of what that organisation does? Put yourself into the shoes of one of your ideal customers, then look at your own website. Does it **really** reflect your brand or products?

Before embarking on any form of marketing strategy, you first need to understand who you are as an organisation, what goals you have and how you would like to be perceived by your target audience(s).

This may involve a certain amount of discussion (even arguments) as well as soul-searching, but if you cannot present a cohesive view of what you are trying to achieve, you cannot expect your customers to buy your product.

If you don't know who you are, nor will your clients!

Most people reading this book will either be in business or will be looking to set up in business. Each of us will have different reasons for doing so, whether it's that we have a burning ambition to be our own boss, we've been forced to through redundancy, or we've simply got an amazing new idea. Whatever the reasons, though, anyone who sets up their own company or is responsible for running a business must have a clear vision for their organisation and what it will be selling.

Putting together a clear vision, a simple mission statement, and developing an understanding of exactly how you wish to be seen by your target audience form the building blocks of any comprehensive marketing strategy and will influence every aspect of your communications with customers. We are now going to walk you through how to define these building blocks for your organisation.

Earlier we mentioned face-to-face networking. As the oldest form of marketing, this still plays a major role in marketing your product or brand. Whether you are at a business pitch, attending an exhibition, meeting friends in a restaurant or speaking at a seminar, you still need to communicate your VKUM – vision, key messages, USPs and mission statement. We'll talk more about each of these in a moment.

Similarly, as your shop window on the world, your website needs to communicate your VKUM for you. The same holds true for your Twitter and Facebook updates, any advertising that you do, or public relations campaign that you embark upon.

So what is a vision?

Entire books have been written on how to define your company's vision. To sum it up, though, the vision can be defined as being the overall strategic long term goal of your company.

Let's consider the following businesses: an organic farmshop in Somerset – **www.pitneyfarmshop.co.uk** – which offers products that are not catered for particularly well by the mainstream supermarkets; a firm of chartered surveyors that offers specific advice for landowners dealing with telecoms operators – **www.batchellerthacker.co.uk/telecoms.html**; and a shop that specialises in vegan shoes – **www.lovethoseshoes.com/vegan-shoes/default.asp**.

All of these businesses have a clear message about what they do, which allows them to know their vision and therefore helps them to attract customers in their appropriate market. On the flip side, though, there are also many people who set up a business without a clear vision for what it is they are trying to achieve. In their haste to set up the company, they don't set defined goals for what that organisation will do. This can lead to confusion about what they wish to achieve and, therefore, what decisions to take.

So, the first step in being able to sell your business and its products is to establish a clear vision. Here are some examples of great vision statements:

Google: "Google's mission is to organize the world's information and make it universally accessible and useful."

McDonald's: "To be our customers' favourite place and way to eat."

Greenpeace: "Our vision is to transform the world by fundamentally changing the way people think about it."

Body Shop: "We believe there is only one way to be beautiful, nature's way."

Ideally you want a short sentence which encapsulates what exactly you are trying to achieve. Not only will this be a good memory hook for you but it will also serve you well in search engine optimisation and even as a line to put on the back of your business cards.

Key messages and USPs

Next you need to define your key messages and what your unique sales propositions or unique selling points (USPs) are. This may take some time and involve doing some research on your competitors as well as due diligence on your marketplace. Obviously very few of us have a *completely* unique product so it is important to focus on what separates you out from your competition – for many companies this will be your staff as they *are* unique.

These key messages and USPs will form the backbone of your marketing and communications strategy so it pays to spend time on getting them right. To assist you in putting these together, it may be helpful to answer these questions:

- **Who**? What sort of organisation are you: company, collective, sole-trader, family business, charity?
- **What**? Exactly what do you do or offer as a service? Just focus on your key offering e.g. selling great value Kenyan coffee.
- **When**? When are your opening hours or when are you available?
- **Where**? What is your location and the geographical area you serve?
- **How**? What way does your company or organisation work?
- **Why**? Why should someone do business with you?

What is your mission statement?

Your company's mission statement explains the purpose of your company to your customers and demonstrates your vision. It also helps you to decide upon which actions to take and what decisions to make. And finally, it gives you a framework within which you can plan your company's future strategy.

Once you have properly identified your vision, key messages and USPs, you can then start to formulate a mission statement which draws together all these themes.

Let's take a hairdressing salon as an example and put together a mission statement for them. We've chosen **www.k2hair.co.uk** in the West Midlands as an example.

What is their vision? Let's assume it is: "To deliver faultless hairdressing services that leave our clients looking and feeling great."

What are their key messages and USPs? By asking some simple questions we can begin to draw these out:

Who? K2 Hair Design.
What? Hairdressing salons.
When? Varying times but sometimes stay open late.
Where? Perton and Codsall.
How? Offer skilled service and professional advice.
Why? Passionate, professional and highly educated. Range of special offers for weddings, children, over 60s and students.

The current mission statement that this company has chosen is:

The k2 company is a team of committed, passionate, professional individuals who willingly give 100% to deliver faultless hairdressing services to the satisfaction of themselves and the k2 client so they want to return again and again.

This is a well developed version of k2's vision. However, it could be improved and made into a more a customer focused mission statement by using a combination of their vision, key messages and USPs (the first three parts of the VKUM). For example:

k2 Hair Design is a Perton and Codsall-based hair salon with a team of committed, passionate, professional individuals providing a range of hairdressing services and advice. Whether you are a bride getting married, a pensioner or a student on a limited wage, k2 will provide a great haircut at a price to suit your budget. We are open late on Thursdays and Fridays.

This should underpin everything you do

When used online, this mission statement should form the basis of your home page. Like a good headline in a newspaper, it will be the first thing that visitors to your website will see. And, as with a good article, the most salient points need to be put across in the least amount of space. Obviously, this information can be expanded in the About Us page later on.

At the same time, as has been done in the revised k2 mission statement above, you need to put as many of the keywords which apply to your business into this piece of text as possible because this will help you in optimising your website for search engines.

How would you like to be seen?

Once you've established a vision and mission statement for your brand or company, this will set the tone for how you wish to be perceived by your target customers. However, this only forms the basis – your job is to build on those foundations to promote your brand to all your audiences.

Therefore, you need to analyse the target markets that you defined in the last chapter closely and try to match their expectations. For example, imagine you were a car restorer based in Cheshire, specialising in 1960s/70s Jaguars and Austin Healey cars and serving just the North West of England. You would tailor your marketing to people living in the main conurbations in and around Greater Manchester, Merseyside, Cheshire, Lancashire and Cumbria; you'd be targeting probably middle aged people with some spare money to invest; many of them would have basic car servicing skills; and they should be within reasonable driving distance of your premises.

Your marketing therefore would reflect your in-depth knowledge and expertise about all aspects of these two types of cars. You would not want to come across as patronising, but more as a helpful consultancy.

Again, as we'll see in a later chapter, this is where Google

AdWords can make such a difference as you can not only specify the search keywords likely to be used by your target market, but also 'negative' keywords that might be used by people you wish to exclude. In this example, you would exclude a host of keywords that didn't relate to the North West of England, Jaguar or Austin Healey.

It is always a good idea to try and visualise your ideal client or clients. Who are they, what would they want from you and why would they want to buy from you? You could go even further than that and look at doing some customer profiling. Use criteria such as age, background, marital status and interests when understanding your client base.

If you want to get proper, independent feedback on what your target markets think about your organisation/product/services, you should consider employing a mystery shopper company such as **www.shopperanonymous.co.uk**.

They can not only help to improve customer service standards but will also give an insight into what your customers think about your marketing by providing you with constructive, non-emotive feedback. They can even improve your sales performance too.

It is always difficult to put yourself into the shoes of your customers as you are too close to your company to give an honest appraisal. However, you may find that the responses you get from a mystery shopper or independent questionnaire will radically change how you market yourself.

A good case study of this is Tulleys Farm (**www.tulleysfarm.com**), a family-run farm shop/attraction near Crawley in West Sussex. They used Shopper Anonymous to provide a mystery shopping programme which touched on all aspects of the business, including the farm shop, the website experience and even calling the business after hours. The feedback was enlightening and improvements were immediate.

Suggested action plan

- Establish what the vision for your company is.

- Establish what the key messages and USPs for your company, brand or products are.

- Prepare a cohesive mission statement that sums up who you are and what you do/sell.

- Use independent sources such as mystery shoppers to help understand how your customers see you.

- Use your vision and mission statement across all of your marketing.

Chapter 7

Creating a comprehensive online marketing strategy

So far, we have outlined the new media landscape and the importance of defining both who you are and who your audiences are. With this in mind, it is now time to move onto creating a strategy which encompasses all aspects of online communications.

As we explained in the second chapter, your website must form the very nucleus of any strategy. Around it are the social media channels which can act either in concert with, or independently of, your website.

However there are a host of other issues that come into play when putting together your strategy – not least the use of search engines. These all need to be factored in to ensure you reach your widest possible target audience for the least amount of marketing spend.

The first step is to focus on your target audience. By now you will have identified who they are and how they consume the media. Your next job is to ascertain what mixture of old and new marketing you will be investing in to reach these people.

So, if you are selling retirement homes in Sussex (**www.stgeorgespark.co.uk**) then the online presence probably won't be as important as traditional media such as Sussex Life, Saga Magazine, the Sunday Telegraph and other lifestyle publications.

On the other hand, if you are selling promotional items over the internet (**www.fatdog.co.uk**) then clearly the online route is going to be the most effective.

There will, however, be many businesses that are going to need to combine the two. For example, an attraction like Chessington World of Adventures (**www.chessington.com**) has a diverse target audience to reach and so will be using the full armoury of marketing tools at its disposal.

It should be clear by now why it is so important that you understand who your target audience is: so as you don't end up wasting money on marketing that is not applicable to your potential customer base.

Looking at your marketing budget

The next step is for you to establish how much money to allocate to your marketing budget. Working out how much you need to be investing in marketing can sometimes be like a chicken and egg situation – until you have allocated a budget, you don't know what you'll be able to afford; but until you have ascertained what media channels you are going to use, you don't know how much you might need to spend.

The keyword here is 'invest' – you are making an investment which is ultimately designed to help drive sales for your business. Therefore, as with any other investment, there needs to be some form of measurable return.

Clearly the advantage of many of the new media marketing tools which we have written about in this book, is that they are free – e.g. Google Analytics, social networking, blogging (if done in-house). In addition, by deciding to ditch traditional or obsolete marketing practices, you may be able to free up funds, thereby maintaining your existing budget or even reducing it.

A key area of spending is on the website. If it is over three years old, it will need replacing, while sites up to two years old may need altering to make them as efficient and optimised as possible. Expect to pay anything from £500 for a basic one-page site, right up to tens of thousands of pounds for a complex, multi-platform site. It is very much a case of cutting your coat to match your cloth.

If you have no real budget, you may wish to consider a Facebook page while you gather together the necessary funding. However, depending on the complexity of your organisation or the products you are wishing to sell, it is perfectly possible to build a website for around £2,000. There are also hosting fees to consider, as well as management fees by the web designer you choose.

However, if you think that the shelf life of a website is 36 months, you are still only paying around £56 per month for your primary marketing tool.

Driving traffic to your website

The second key cost can be search marketing – paying to ensure you maximise traffic to your website. There are three keys ways that you can drive traffic to your website.

1) 'Organically' through regular content management of your website using blogs, social media, and advertising your website URL using traditional marketing techniques
2) Search engine optimisation (SEO) which helps you get to the top of the page in the search engines' natural results, and
3) Google AdWords (or a similar pay-per-click advertising system) where you pay for visitors from sponsored ads that appear to the right-hand-side or at the top of the Google search page.

Three steps to website heaven

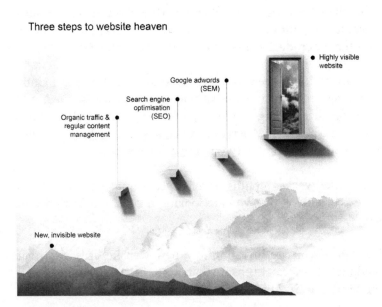

Let's look at each of these methods in more detail:

Organic traffic and content management

As we have previously pointed out earlier in the book, one of the cheapest and easiest ways to drive traffic to your site is by using blogs and social media.

Don't forget too that email signatures, word of mouth, business cards and traditional advertising are also great ways to push people through to websites.

However, these options need to be used in conjunction with either SEO or Google AdWords to maximise the amount of traffic you get.

Search engine optimisation

The second way to drive people to your website is search engine optimisation. This can be defined as 'the process of doing things to the content, structure, and underlying architecture of your website so that the search engines see it as a worthwhile and authoritative site containing information which is highly relevant to the search terms that your ideal visitors are likely to enter into Google'.

SEO can cost anywhere between £100 and £10,000 per month, depending on how competitive your marketplace is. Clearly, it will be far cheaper to get to the top of the organic search rankings if you are a florist in Abergavenny (**www.hilarysflowers.co.uk**) than if you are in London (**www.arenaflowers.com**).

It may take weeks, months or even years until you can obtain the search ranking that you are looking for (i.e. the first page of Google, Bing or Yahoo).

However, if you are investing in a new website, it is vital that you do what you can to ensure that, from the start, the site is well optimised. This includes:

- Incorporating the correct keywords for your brand or product into the content of the site
- Choosing a keyword rich domain name
- Using keyword rich file names for each of your site's pages
- Having multiple pages of optimised content for each of your chosen keywords
- Ensuring your site can be easily crawled by search engine 'spiders' (programs that scour the web reading the content of everyone's websites)
- Making correct use of <title> tags and ensuring they contain your keywords – your web designer should be able to assist you with this
- Getting links to your site from other relevant websites including the major directory sites

However, a word of warning. It is not generally a good idea to attempt SEO yourself as it takes a lot of effort, time and experience. Just as you wouldn't try and service a high performance sports car after going on a basic car maintenance course, you shouldn't try and understand the highly technical way in which websites are optimised.

Google AdWords (pay-per-click advertising)

The third, and far more cost effective approach, is to use pay-per-click (PPC) advertising systems such as Google AdWords to drive people to your website. With PPC, adverts for your website appear on Google, or other search engines, in response to relevant searches. As the advertiser, you **only** pay if your advert is clicked.

Simply put, this is the 21st Century approach to advertising and neatly espouses the modern approach to marketing that we have been championing in this book. It's about putting your ad in front of people who are actually looking for what you offer (rather than using an 'outbound' or scattergun approach) and only paying for a positive response.

In the diagram below, the difference between Google's natural results and the AdWords results is clearly illustrated. The area we've highlighted with a dotted outline contains the natural/organic results (achieved using SEO) while the two areas to which we've applied a solid outline contain the paid-for AdWords search results.

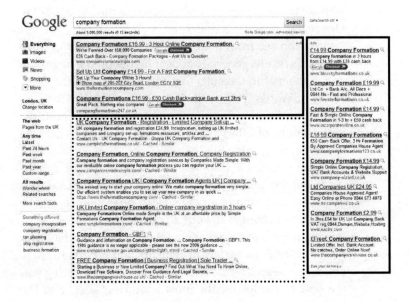

A good example of how powerful AdWords can be is Joanna Parker and her professional catering company **www.joannaparker.co.uk** in Gloucestershire. Like many people in business, Joanna believed that new business would automatically be boosted once a website was set up but, as she found out, this doesn't always happen.

However, after having a Google AdWords campaign set up for her to help boost visitor numbers to the website, Joanna saw a 300% rise in enquiries in just a couple of months. This led to a massive increase in new business and gave her a total return on her advertising investment of 468%!

While both SEO and AdWords definitely offer a way to positively boost the online presence of any business, we believe that AdWords is usually the better alternative. Some of the key benefits you get from using Google AdWords are:

- It offers **instant** results – with your website being listed on page one of Google typically within 24 hours. This means that from the day an AdWords campaign is set up, any business or client can see an immediate increase in website traffic, whereas it takes time for the use of SEO to kick in and produce a return.
- As you can see from the earlier screenshot, the top three AdWords results generally appear higher up the page than any of the 'natural' results that are achieved with SEO.
- With AdWords your website can appear in Google's search results for a huge range of keywords, without the vast amount of effort that would be required to achieve the same thing using SEO.
- Amendments to a Google AdWords campaign can be made quickly and easily. This means that if, for example, you want to promote a new special offer, you can make the required changes to your ads straightaway.
- It is really easy to see what's working well and what isn't. AdWords offers a variety of statistics and reports to show you which search terms and which ads are generating you the best traffic levels, the most enquiries/sales, and the best return on your investment.

- You can set a budget and stick to it. With AdWords you can keep on top of the finances by limiting the cost per click and the total daily spend.

Because AdWords is so powerful, we will be going into much more detail on it and explaining more about how to use it in Chapter 9.

Look at all the available social media

In this book, we have mainly focused on the four key social networking sites – Facebook, LinkedIn, Twitter and YouTube. However there are over 750 other social networking sites which can be investigated (**http://bit.ly/f97OaO**).

It is important to look at your target markets and ascertain exactly which social media is most applicable to your business. The following guidelines will help you:

- Facebook is very much a business to consumer (B2C) tool and is useful if you are trying to reach out directly to your marketplace, as well as building your brand online. Good examples of this are hotels, pubs, shops and restaurants. Facebook is not really applicable as a business to business tool (B2B) e.g. an engineering firm supplying the car industry.
- LinkedIn is all about online networking and brand building, making it very much a B2B tool. Using the engineering firm in the last bullet point as an example, they can network with other suppliers, seek out potential new markets, enhance their reputation and share best practice.
- Twitter may on the surface be seen as a B2C sales tool but it is in fact also used as an online networking tool or a way to advertise your brand or services to a wide audience. Recruitment consultants can advertise jobs, shops can post special deals, and professional services firms can talk about important issues affecting their sector. It is also a great way of finding suppliers and affiliate partners.
- YouTube is both a B2C and B2B tool. If you want to

communicate your brand visually through video, this is the perfect way to reach your customers e.g. hotels, estate agents, leisure attractions, holiday homes, etc. At the same time, it can be used as an educational tool or as a way of illustrating how things work. For example, training videos for operatives of forklift trucks could be uploaded or footage of a component for an industrial shredder being assembled.

- Ecademy is very similar to LinkedIn and is a way to network online and build your brand.
- Wikipedia can be utilised if you have a well-known brand, own an historic building or attraction, or even work in a famous place, in as much that there is scope for you to create or amend the relevant Wikipedia entry and add a link to your website. A good example would be something like Chatsworth House (**http://en.wikipedia.org/wiki/Chatsworth_House**) where the article has a number of useful resources listed.
- Amazon can provide you, as an approved seller, with your own storefront or page on the site which you can use to sell products. However, you will not be able to list your own website.
- eBay works in a similar way to Amazon in that, as a seller of items, you can have your own presence on the site.
- Flickr (**www.flickr.com**) does for photos what YouTube does for videos, so if your product or service is very visual – e.g. photographers, artists, interior designers – this can be a great way to share photos that will display your work to a wide audience.
- MySpace (**www.myspace.com**) can, for anyone working in the arts, act in much the same way as Facebook. It launched the career of Lily Allen amongst others.

Once you have decided which of the above are most appropriate for your business, you should set up a direct link to these sites from your website and publicise the appropriate links on business cards, email signatures, etc.

Autoresponders

Once you have driven traffic to your website and filled it with interesting and relevant content, you need to build a relationship with your customer – just as you would if they walked into your shop or called up to ask about your consultancy services.

One of the simplest and most effective ways in which to do this is to set up an autoresponder system, which is something that can help automate part of this relationship building process.

However, before we talk about why autoresponders are so powerful, we firstly need to understand something about the way people buy. There are three important points here:

1. People buy from people that they have got to know and come to trust
2. People are more likely to buy from a 'trusted adviser' than they are from a 'salesman'
3. People rarely buy on the first contact with you or your company

Think about it. How many times have you come across a business or its website for the very first time and immediately spent a significant amount of money with them? Probably never. Most of us start off just doing some research and looking for information and it takes a few days/weeks/months until we are ready to buy. Yet most businesses don't bother going back to their potential customers and following up on the initial conversation because they don't want to appear 'pushy'.

Imagine though what might happen if you did keep in regular contact with your prospective customers. Come that time a few days/weeks/months later when they were eventually ready to buy, which company would they be most likely to go back to in order to make that purchase? Would it be (a) the one that had been keeping in regular contact with them, or (b) one of the many others that had not bothered to do any kind of follow-up?

Assuming you answered (a), the next question is how do you keep in regular contact with your prospects without looking pushy and without taking up loads and loads of your time?

The answer is simple. You use an autoresponder service to send a series of pre-written emails containing useful information (not a barrage of sales messages) to your prospects automatically on a regular basis.

The reason this is so great is that it gives you leverage. In other words, it allows you to do a piece of work once and then re-use it time and time again without any extra effort on your part. This means that setting up an autoresponder will give you a very good return on the investment of your time that's involved (or on the money that you pay someone else to set it up for you).

With an autoresponder, potential customers subscribe to a mailing list and are then automatically sent a pre-written series of emails, with a preset time interval between each message. They join this mailing list by filling in a simple form. Once they've done this, they receive an email asking them to confirm that they really did want to join the list. This is called a double opt-in and is used to guard against the possibility of someone entering someone else's details on the signup form instead of their own (either deliberately or accidentally).

Once the potential customer has confirmed their subscription they then start to receive the series of emails that you have written. It doesn't matter when they sign up. They will always start off with message number one, then a few days later they'll get message number two, then a while later they'll get number three, and so on. It's up to you to specify what the time interval is between each message. You might, for example, send message two a couple of days after the first message, then wait a week before sending message number three.

The main thing is that over a period of time, your prospective customer will get a series of regular emails from you, each one giving them a bit of useful relevant information and reminding them that you exist. And that means when they are ready to buy, they are likely to think of you – the person who has been there giving them handy free information every few days for the past month or so.

The big question is what do you put in these emails. Well for a start it has to be content that won't go out-of-date quickly. Once you've written your series of emails, you want to be able to re-use them every time a new person joins your mailing list, so you need content that will be accurate and of interest for some time to come and you need to avoid anything seasonal (e.g. information related to Christmas).

You also need to make sure the information you send to people via an autoresponder is relevant and of interest to them. And note that we say to *them* – because if it's only of interest and relevance to you and not to your potential customers, then few peoples are going to sign up to receive your emails. And those that do sign up are likely to unsubscribe pretty quickly. Think back to our earlier chapter where we talked about the importance of identifying your target markets.

Usually the nature of your business and/or the topic of your website will give you a big steer as to what to write about in your autoresponder emails. For example, if you run a golf shop a good theme for your autoresponder emails might be some tips and advice on how to play better golf. This will almost certainly be of interest to your website visitors and is the kind of information which will be as accurate and relevant in a year's time as it is today.

Another thing is to remember your VKUM – vision, key messages, USP and mission. These should always be included. But if you really struggle to write the content yourself, there are plenty of copywriters who can do it for you.

Having decided what your follow-up emails will be about, the next challenge is to get people to sign up. You do NOT want your website visitors to sign up to a newsletter. People aren't interested in your 'news' – they want something that they perceive to be of value to them.

A good strategy is to offer them a free report. And give it a punchy headline so people take notice of it. Use phrases like *'learn the secrets of....'*, *'download our top tips for....'*, etc that will entice people to want to read the information you're offering.

So for the golf shop referred to earlier, you could have a prominent box somewhere on the site with a headline *'Top ten tips for the perfect putt'* and then a little note explaining that all they have to do is enter their name and email address and they'll receive these free tips on how to improve their putting. And a headline like that will then naturally determine the number and content of the autoresponder emails – in this case a series of ten emails, each giving a tip or piece of advice on how to get better at putting.

Here is an example of an autoresponder signup form on the Divadani Design website (**www.divadanidesign.com**)

Think about how this may affect HR policy within your organisation

Clearly, these changes in marketing will affect both your existing staff as well as influencing how to recruit new personnel.

In the short term, it may be worth identifying members of staff who could potentially be trained up to manage your news page and social media sites. Very often it will be younger members of your team who (a) are more willing to learn new skills (b) are at home with social media and (c) cost far less than employing expensive external consultants.

At the same time, if you do employ external marketing or public relations consultants, find out how familiar they are with the new forms of marketing. If they are not, you may wish to find new consultants. Alternatively, if they are *au fait* with online marketing, you could ask them to change the services they provide. For example, a retained PR agency could update your news page for you instead of liaising with the media.

In the medium term, and depending on how proactive you wish to be, it may be worth employing someone to perform the old in-house press officer/marketing assistant role. Instead of promoting stories to the press, their job would be to monitor the social media accounts, update the news page and gather stories from within your organisation.

In the same way that a host of agencies sprang up in the 1980s and 1990s specialising in public relations, marketing, branding, etc, the next decade will see the emergence of new companies which will focus specifically on the new, online media. Therefore we forecast consultancies which will just handle Facebook or Twitter, video production companies that assist with YouTube (there are already many – **www.macmillion.com** and **www.endorfin.tv** to name but two) and news agencies which will cater for companies' blogging needs.

Therefore in the long term, there will be cost implications involved either in taking on outside agencies or employing specialists in-house to manage your online marketing.

Being proactive

The only way any of your online marketing will be effective is if you are totally committed to it and are as proactive as you can be.

Traditionally, many companies would spend money on marketing and hope that it would work – running advertising campaigns, sending out mailshots, employing PR agencies, very often without having any mechanisms to test and measure how effective each of these marketing tools was.

Now it is less a case of just investing money and more about using your brain and being creative with your marketing. However, if you do not update your website, you do not constantly check your analytics, you do not increase your social media fan base, you do not network and you do not have a strategy for generating traffic via search engines, you will struggle.

Suggested action plan

- Look closely at the vision, key messages, USP and mission statement (VKUM) for your company.

- Establish which marketing channels you are going to use to communicate with your target audiences.

- Make sure your website is effective as it can be.

- Formulate a marketing budget which will include the cost of driving traffic to your website.

- Investigate setting up autoresponders on your website.

- Review HR policy, in terms of marketing.

- BE PROACTIVE!!!!!!

Chapter 8

Making sure your website is fit for purpose

You've now got a marketing strategy with a website (or, should funds be limited, a Facebook page) sitting at the heart. Your aim now is to ensure that it is up to the job of driving all your marketing tools.

As we explained earlier, websites have come on a huge amount over the past fifteen years while costs have dropped markedly. Therefore, while the capital expense may appear high, when looked at in the medium and long term against other marketing costs, a website can offer an excellent and cost effective return on your investment.

To highlight the role of a great website, we would say that it should do as good a job of selling your products or brand as if you were in the room with a potential client, selling to them face-to-face. In an ideal world, your website is a highly skilled salesperson, marketing you to your target audience 24/7. Therefore it must be the best that YOU can afford.

If you are planning a brand new website, just setting up in business or are thinking about overhauling your existing site, you need to think about the following:

Purpose and target audience

Going back to the VKUM principle you really need to understand who your target audience is and how you would like to come across to them. Also, you need to understand the purpose of the site. Different sites have different delineated roles. What would you like yours to be for? Is it there to:

- Provide information/act as online brochure?
- Generate enquiries/sales leads?
- Build a mailing list?
- Give credibility?
- Build brand awareness?
- Sell things using e-commerce?
- All of the above?

Good design

The same principles that are at work in traditional marketing – brochures, advertisements, hoardings, shop windows – apply equally in an online setting. However good a website may be structurally, if it doesn't look appealing then people will not stay on it for very long. A site that looks like it was thrown together by an amateur will not make people think you are a professional business and will not make them feel confident about trusting you to deliver whatever product or service it is they are looking for.

As with any form of written text, be it a newspaper article, brochure or blog, it must be easy to read. Large blocks of text or small fonts make it difficult for people to read and they will 'bounce' away from your site quickly. It also goes without saying that the site – particularly your home page – should be both interesting and pertinent to all your target markets.

Landing pages

There may be times when you have various different target markets, in which case you may wish to think about creating a number of dedicated landing pages, one for each type of visitor. A landing page is simply the specific page of your website that a particular visitor arrives at when they first enter your website. In many cases this will be your home page, but it could just as well be any other page of your site that has been built specifically as the entry point for one particular target audience.

By using links to specific landing pages in your online and offline marketing, you can ensure that you send potential customers to the part of your website which is most likely to be relevant and of interest to them, thus increasing the chances of them becoming a customer.

For example, if you are an osteopath who specialises in cranial osteopathy for babies but you also cater for people with workplace-related back problems, you have clearly got two different target audiences and so you may want to think about designing two different landing pages. One landing page will provide details of your cranial osteopathy services for babies and the other will talk about how you can help cure workplace-related back problems. But the ultimate purpose of both pages will be to get visitors to book an appointment, and the pages will include appropriate calls to action to achieve this.

Clear layout

Following on from the need for good design, websites must be clear and accessible. With attention spans becoming ever shorter, the simpler a website is, the more likely people are to read it. Think in terms of newspaper layout – papers have developed over the past 300 years into something that readers can access news from in minutes, with easy menus and bold headlines to catch the eye.

Easy to use – for you and your visitors

Like a good instruction booklet, the table of contents in a magazine, or a road map, your website must be easy to navigate. Too many subheadings, confusing menus or buried links will make a site inaccessible. Realistically you should be able to access all salient pages with just two clicks of a mouse.

A lot of websites still try to force people to watch an animated Flash presentation before they can get into the main part of the website. The thing is, visitors to your site don't want to watch them – so they'll click the Back button instead.

Many sites also include background music and sound effects – don't do it; unwanted music and noises are highly irritating.

At the same time, it must be simple for you or your staff to use. In other words, it should have an intuitive content management system. Gone are the days when you had to liaise with a web designer and pay through the nose to get even small alterations to your site. With the introduction of software like Wordpress, websites are as easy to update as a Facebook page.

In the design phase, you can specify how much of your site you would like control over so changes can be made very quickly, for no cost at all. This makes it ideal for people who want to change text and images on a regular basis. However, you do still need a designer if you wish to make structural changes.

The key thing here is control. For far too long, companies had little control over their own websites and were unwilling to make too many changes for fear of how much it would cost. Now that is no longer an issue and websites will be all the better for it.

Strong call-to-action

Your site must serve a purpose – i.e. getting visitors to lift the phone, subscribe to a mailing list or book an appointment. Too many websites simply describe the company or product without actually urging visitors to do anything.

Generally speaking you need to have a phone number, email address, or access to social networking sites in the top right hand corner of the page.

Credibility

Visitors to your site should be also able to find your full postal address, company registration number, VAT number, phone, email, terms & conditions, privacy policy, etc easily. Making this information freely available boosts your credibility, increases trust, and is in some cases a legal requirement.

Watch what you say

Many companies fall into the trap of using jargon or forgetting who they are trying to communicate with. Remember who your customer is and use language appropriate to them. For example, a web developer should avoid talking at length about the technical features of websites, content management systems, programming languages, etc because their target audience will be completely confused by this and will simply want to know how the web developer can assist them in building a website that works for their company.

When writing content for your website there are a number of points to bear in mind:

- It is imperative that you focus on the benefits, NOT the features of your product or service
- Where possible give a guarantee or list testimonials from satisfied customers
- Make your website customer focused
- Have effective headlines – using the Attention, Interest, Desire, Action principle – see **http://www.mindtools.com/pages/article/AIDA.htm** for more on this
- Your text should be like the perfect skirt – long enough to cover all the essentials yet short enough to be interesting!

Plenty of traffic

Once you've got a website that is up to the job, you want to maximise the number of visitors to it by ensuring it is easy to find on search engines. No matter how good a website is, without being particularly search friendly, it is invisible.

A study by ClickScene in March 2011 found that 40% of UK websites get no visitors at all (**bit.ly/hzL5C8**). It's like having a phone but not giving anyone the number or listing it in any phone directory – you'll never get called. From the outset, you need to work with a web designer who understands search engine optimisation. If they don't, we recommend getting in an SEO or PPC specialist.

It follows, then, that your goal is to get close to the top of the search engines for your key search terms. Depending on your business, this may be quite hard to achieve using SEO – for example if you are an hotel in London or a pub in Blackpool – in which case, this is where Google AdWords comes into its own.

However, for many businesses, some simple optimisation when the site is built, along with regular content management, will often make it possible to get on the first page of Google.

Make the most of every visitor

The next stage in the process is to ensure that as many visitors as possible coming to the site become customers – i.e. you need to start building a relationship with them. This is where things like blogs and autoresponders come into play.

Reflect the character and personalities of your organisation and your staff

One of the advantages of modern websites is that it is now possible to build a more three-dimensional picture of both your company, products and personnel. Gone are the days when your website was a static set of pages which gave very little clue about the human beings who worked behind the brand. People deal with people, and in any customer-focused or professional services industry, clients and customers want to get a good idea about who they are dealing with.

Any 'about us' or biography section could have videos of key members of staff, direct access to their LinkedIn profiles plus personal testimonials from former clients or colleagues. This will reveal more about the personalities of key personnel.

For example, a recruitment agency may have a very good brand name. However, new clients will want to know that they are dealing with an experienced recruiter rather than someone who's only been in the job five minutes.

Regularly updated and highly visible news page

As mentioned earlier, it is vital to put as much fresh copy onto your website as you can – not only to build your brand but also to boost your position on search engines. This will form the heart of your social media platform too as the news page will feed sites like Twitter and Facebook automatically.

Generally speaking, the news page should be clearly labelled in the menu on the home page or, even better, there should be a live feed on the home page. Some companies even include their Twitter and Facebook updates on the home page too, as this just adds extra content and helps to boost their brand or products further.

News pages are very often in the top ten of pages viewed by visitors and, especially if your news items also appear on the home page, they are the best way to reinforce your key messages and USPs on a regular basis.

A note of caution though – if you really don't think anyone in your organisation is willing or able to update this page, or you don't have the funds available to pay someone else to do it, then don't have a news page. Although not having a news page will be detrimental to your marketing effort, it is better to do without one altogether than have a news page which is never updated.

Cross-browser and cross-device friendly

Although Internet Explorer remains the most commonly used web browser, there are lots of people using other popular browsers such as Firefox, Safari and Chrome. So you need to ensure that your website displays correctly and functions properly in *all* the major web browsers, not just the one that you happen to use yourself.

In addition, you must be aware of the constantly evolving shift away from people accessing the internet via desktop and laptop computers. With the advent of smartphones and tablet devices, the free availability of wifi, and the evolution of 3G and 4G technology, more and more people will choose to view web pages on the move from handheld devices.

Clearly then your site must be optimised for this technology. If you want your website to be easily accessible by people using mobile devices you need to remember the following:

- Black backgrounds should be avoided as they are difficult to see on an iPhone or Blackberry
- Your site should not use Flash animations and effects as Flash can't currently be displayed by Apple products – iPhones, iPods or iPads

- Pages need to fit into the browser easily as people often can't be bothered to scroll down. If your pages are too long or too wide, important parts of your website may be entirely missed by many visitors.

There is also coding which can be put into your website which means that the look of it changes, depending on the browser or device you are using. In other words, you can display a different version of your website to someone who is accessing it via a mobile phone.

This means, for example, that companies using e-commerce or offering an in-depth search facility (recruiters, travel agents, estate agents, etc) can by default just offer mobile phone users a much simplified search facility plus the call to action, rather than risk overloading them with the full version of the website. A good example of this is IKEA (**www.ikea.co.uk**). Many news sites (**www.bbc.co.uk/news**, **www.guardian.co.uk**) do this too, as well as train operating companies.

Google Analytics embedded

The single most important marketing measurement tool MUST be on your site from the very first day it goes live. Or if you have an existing site, get it embedded as quickly as you can.

Without it, you are very much in the dark as to how your site is performing.

Flexible enough to be updated without major costs

Imagine that you want a three bedroom house built for you and your family – a domestic set-up of two parents, two kids. You hire an architect to design you one, then a builder to construct it. Two years after you move in, you decide you want another child and therefore need a fourth bedroom. You then have to commission the builder to reconfigure the existing house so you can add the extra room. It would have been far most cost effective to have a four bed house built in the first place, even if you didn't use the fourth bedroom.

So it is with websites. Although you can never fully future-proof your website, you can plan ahead and work out whether at some stage in the next one, two, or three years you may want to add pages. Better to do it at the planning stage than down the line when changes may prove costly or, in extreme cases, you have to rebuild your website from scratch.

This is particularly applicable to new businesses or companies that find themselves selling to a different marketplace. When planning your business goals for the coming years, you need to think about whether your website will be able to grow with you.

Be something you are really proud of!

This may appear to be common sense but so many companies still have websites they are ashamed to show people. Considering this is your shop window on the world, this could be costly. Whatever marketing you do, be it face-to-face, social networking or PR, you must be really proud of your site as it will give you the confidence to sell your brand and products more effectively. Get it wrong, and all this effort could well be in vain.

Writing a website brief

You should by now have a very clear idea about what you would **like** your website to do as well as what it **must** do. Now you need to communicate these ideas in a clear form of words so you can hire a web designer to turn them into reality.

You will often hear companies moan about their website, blaming it on the web designers who built it for them. The reality is that the brief was probably where the problem lay.

It would be true to say that if you give a bad brief to a good web designer, you may end up with a sub-standard website. However, if the reverse was true and you gave a well-written, concise brief to an average designer, the chances are that you would still get the site you wanted.

Conveying your vision for your website is like speaking to an interior designer before giving your home a make-over. It is vital that you help the designer understand exactly what you have in mind.

To assist in this process, prepare a simple document that outlines the following:

- Your VKUM – vision, key messages, USPs and mission statement – as this will give them an exact idea of who you are and what you do
- As much salient information about your company, your staff, products, services and target markets as possible
- Background on the company
- Information on your key clients
- How you wish to use your existing branding online – logo, corporate colours, fonts, etc
- The level of access that you or other members of staff will need to the site
- Your available budget

It would also be worth looking at some competitor websites, (a) to understand how they market themselves and (b) to come up with something fresh that marks you out as different.

Finally, you should look at a range of websites that you really like in order to establish in your mind what works for you. To use the interior designer analogy again, you would need to know what colours and textures you liked before engaging the services of the designer.

Armed with all of these in a two or three page brief, you would then be able to send the brief to a selection of web designers, inviting them to tender. Or you could simply give it to your existing designer, if you have a good working relationship with them.

Working with web designers

Like a man's relationship with his tailor or a woman's relationship with her hairdresser, it is important to get on with your web designer – only if they are up to the job of course! They have the ability to turn your ideas into reality and to help you achieve your marketing aims. And, like tailors or hairdressers, sometimes their role is to challenge you and guide you in directions that you may not have considered previously.

Therefore, if you currently use a web designer, then I would advise retaining their services, unless they are patently unable to deliver your brief or do not have the requisite understanding of modern online marketing, as set out in this book.

If however you don't currently use a web designer or are thinking of getting in someone fresh to look at your branding and marketing, you need to find at least three reputable and, if possible, local companies who you can invite to tender.

For those businesses who don't have any contacts with local web designers, you have several channels available to you:

- Word of mouth – through your local business network, ask other companies who they have used in the past.
- Google – simply put in your geographical location and the term 'web designer' and see who comes up. Look at their websites, see if they have any testimonials and establish whether they have a decent social media presence. This is exactly the same process as you would expect your customers to use to find you online, so it is useful practice.
- Business networking – attend a local networking group such as BNI or 4Networking. Many will have web designers in them. If not, one of the members will almost certainly have the contact details for one.
- Advertise for one via LinkedIn or Twitter.

Once you have a set of names, whittle them down to a shortlist of three. People you do NOT want to use are web programmers who are trying their hand at designing, designers who are trying to do some web development work, and 'Jack of all trades' people who say they can do everything – design, build, SEO, AdWords, copywriting, etc. As the saying goes, they will be master of none of these specialist areas.

Of course, there are many good companies with a *team* of people, each specialising in one of these different areas, but you can't expect a one-man band to be able to handle all these things.

Be slightly wary of web designers who outsource everything to countries such as India or the Philippines. While it is perfectly acceptable to outsource some of the web development and other technical work to these countries, you need to have a main point of contact closer to home who you can meet face-to-face, in case anything goes wrong.

Once you have the shortlist of web designers, send them the website brief, along with a deadline for submissions. It is also helpful at this stage to establish roughly what budget you have available so the designers can try and match their proposals accordingly. You can either request that they email you their proposals and costings or, preferably, set aside a time when they can come in to present to you. That way you can establish whether they are people you are going to be able to get along with.

It is then a case of choosing the designer who you think is most capable of translating your brief into reality and who you think you could establish a good working relationship with. The reason for this is that once they've delivered your website, you need to have an on-going dialogue about how best to update it, add new features, etc.

The next step is to engage the services of the web designer or agency. They will usually ask for half their fee up front and will request the remainder on completion of the job. Also, try to put in a deadline for when you want the work completed, or it could (and does!) drag on for months. Generally speaking, from first instructing an agency to the website going live takes around three months, depending on how hands-on you are as a client and how complex you want your new website to be.

After a few weeks, the designer will come back with their first ideas – 'mood boards' showing different mock-ups of the home page, along with a site map. The idea is that you choose the style that comes closest to your ideal and the designer goes away and works with this – or not, if you don't like what they've done of course!

Eventually you'll have a working design of the home page and a pretty good idea about the structure of the new site. Your job now will be to provide the copy to go on the website, as well as high quality visuals. This is where you must go back to your marketing plan and refer back to your key messages. You also need to establish what your keywords are so they can be dropped into the copy to go on your new pages. Last but not least, you need to set yourself a timetable as delays can quickly start occurring if you haven't set proper deadlines.

If there is no one in your organisation who is capable of writing crisp, search-friendly copy, we would recommend taking on a copywriter (use the same process in finding one as you did with the web designer). As long as you can give them a working draft of the words you want to go up, they will quickly and inexpensively provide you with well-written, SEO-friendly copy. And you'll get your website finished much quicker as a result.

At the same time, you need to ensure that you have high quality images, which will do justice to your new website. Nowhere is this more important than on the pages where you have photos of your staff. As with social media, the way your personnel come across online is critical. There are however specialist photographers (e.g. **www.bothhemispheres.com**) who can ensure you and your staff appear in the best possible light. If you need to display images of your products on your website, these photos should be taken by a professional photographer too.

The final stage of your website build is where the web designer will send you a 'beta' version of your new site – essentially it works but is not live, allowing you to make changes to it or test its usability on key members of staff within your organisation. This duly done, you sign off the site and up it goes.

All you have to do now is create a buzz about your new site using all the techniques we have outlined in previous chapters such as word of mouth, networking, social media, email signatures, direct mail and business cards.

Moving your website forward

You now have a website which is well optimised, looks good and is something you're really proud of. What next? How are you going to drive the maximum number of visitors to it?

We previously mentioned the three ways to generate traffic – regular content management, search engine optimisation, and AdWords. However, there are also things you can do to improve your conversion rate – i.e. to ensure that as many of your visitors as possible make a purchase, call you, or submit an enquiry.

One sure-fire way to increase your conversion rate is to offer some kind of guarantee. You see, one of the challenges you face as a business when you try to sell or generate enquiries via the web is that very often there is no face-to-face contact. So it becomes even harder than it is in 'real life' to build up trust in you and your company. And without trust, a potential customer is unlikely to buy from you.

By offering a guarantee you help your potential customer overcome their fear that something will go wrong and that means they are more likely to trust you enough to buy from you. This guarantee can take various forms, depending on the nature of your business – for example:

- We guarantee delivery before midday. If we deliver late we'll refund your delivery charge.
- We guarantee you won't find this product cheaper

anywhere else. If you do we'll refund the difference.
- We guarantee if we can't come up with a design you like we'll refund you in full.
- 100% satisfaction guaranteed or your money back.

Whatever kind of guarantee you opt for in your business, it is essential that you have it clearly displayed on your website. Your guarantee is going to be a vital tool in helping you get more enquiries via your website, so don't hide it away in the smallprint. Shout about it wherever you can on your site.

Obviously, from your customers' point of view, this final one from the list of examples above is the most powerful guarantee and the one that is most likely to convince them to do business with you rather than one of your competitors.

But a lot of businesses are reluctant to offer such a wide-ranging guarantee in case it ends up costing them money. In reality, though, unless you've got a useless product or you offer bad customer service on a regular basis, this kind of guarantee will increase your profits rather than lose you money.

What worries a lot of business owners is the fear that if they offer a no quibble money back guarantee then everyone will take advantage of that and ask for their money back even when they were completely happy. But in reality this doesn't happen because most people are basically pretty honest. The vast majority of your customers will only invoke that guarantee if they are genuinely unhappy with your service.

Do you often have really unhappy customers in your business? If not, then you have nothing to fear from offering a cast-iron guarantee and publishing it on your website. Even if a few dishonest customers do take advantage of you, the money you lose on them will be far outweighed by all the extra sales you make as a result of offering a guarantee.

Suggested action plan

- Make sure your website is up to the job and you allocate sufficient resources to make it the very best you can afford.

- Think about what you would like it to do, as well as what it should be doing – include your VKUM.

- Prepare a detailed website brief.

- Don't use the first web designer you come across – there will be dozens in your area, all of varying abilities and price ranges.

- Work closely with your designer to achieve the site you want.

- Be proactive and use autoresponders, guarantees and AdWords to build traffic to your site and increase conversions.

Chapter 9

Driving traffic to your website with AdWords

If you are really serious about getting new business from the internet then you are going to need to get involved with pay per click (PPC) sooner rather than later, even if you manage to become an expert in SEO. But, equally, if you venture into pay per click without knowing what you are doing, you could very easily throw a whole load of money down the drain.

However, if you take the time to learn about PPC before you rush headlong into setting up your first campaign (or if you decide to get it done for you by a specialist), then you have the potential to generate large volumes of traffic to your website, and hence create profits, in return for a minimal advertising outlay.

What is pay per click?

First, let's talk about what we mean by pay per click advertising and how it works.

As we touched on earlier, pay per click adverts are the ones that appear down the right hand side of the screen (and often above the main search results too) on search engines such as Google, Yahoo, Bing, etc. They appear under a heading such as "Sponsored Links" and there are usually about ten adverts per page of search results.

The first successful PPC programme was launched by a company called GoTo in 1998. GoTo offered advertisers the opportunity to place bids in an attempt to appear at the top of the results pages for specific search engine queries.

So, for example, an estate agent in Notting Hill might decide to bid £1 in the hope of appearing at the top of the search results whenever someone searched for *'property for sale London'*.

If more than one advertiser bid on the same search term then the order in which the ads appeared was determined by the amount bid. So, an advertiser who bid £1 for the search term *'property for sale London'* would appear higher up the listings than someone who only bid 90p.

Whatever amount the advertiser had bid would be charged each time someone clicked on their advert. This was the key thing that marked out pay per click from the other forms of online advertising which had gone before it. Previously, with things like banner advertising, charges were made according to the number of impressions – i.e. how often the advert was shown to people. But with PPC there are no charges for an advert being shown; there is only a charge if and when the advert is clicked on once it has been displayed.

The basic principle of pay per click programmes has remained the same ever since. *However, contrary to popular belief, the bid price is no longer the only thing that determines what order the adverts appear in.* We'll talk more about this a bit later.

GoTo later renamed itself to Overture and began providing the PPC advertising for major search engines such as Yahoo and MSN Search (the forerunner to Bing). Yahoo liked Overture's service so much that they bought Overture in 2003 and eventually rebranded it as Yahoo Search Marketing.

Meanwhile, Google had set up its own PPC system called Google AdWords which offered a much greater range of features than Overture. Microsoft then launched its own Microsoft AdCenter to power the PPC advertising on its search engine. This was very similar to Google AdWords in terms of its features and appearance.

Yahoo Search Marketing and Microsoft AdCenter continue to exist today (albeit in a merged form), but Google AdWords has emerged as the dominant player, mainly by virtue of the fact that Google has such a large share of the search engine marketplace and is the first port of call for most people when they want to find something on the web.

For that reason, it is the Google AdWords pay per click advertising system which we will be purely focusing on throughout the rest of this chapter.

So, how do you set up a successful pay per click advertising campaign?

Broadly speaking, there are four things you need to get right in order to get the best out of AdWords: your advert, your keywords, your bid prices and your landing pages.

Keywords

Your keywords are the words and phrases that you are going to bid on – i.e. the things that the potential visitors to your website might be typing into Google as search terms. So, a list of keywords for the Notting Hill estate agent in our earlier example might look like this:

- estate agent London
- property for sale London
- houses for sale London
- flats for sale London
- real estate London
- buy property London

If you set up your AdWords campaign with the above list of keywords, then your advert would potentially appear whenever someone typed one of those phrases into Google.

The next thing you need is an advert. This will need to follow the same kind of format as all the other sponsored search results that appear on Google. That means you will need a title of up to 25 characters followed by two lines of text (max 35 characters each) and then a line that contains the URL of your website.

So, an advert for our estate agent in Notting Hill might look like this:

> London Estate Agent
> Wide range of flats and houses
> to buy or rent. Friendly service.
> www.somewebsite.com

And the final thing to do is decide how much to bid. If you enter a bid price, then Google will give you an estimate of where your advert will appear in the rankings for that level of bid. So, you might find that if you entered a bid price of £2 per click that your advert was estimated to appear in positions one to three for your chosen keywords. On that basis, you might decide to go with a bid price of £2 per click.

If you are a London-based estate agent, then hopefully you *haven't* been following this step-by-step and setting up your own campaign in this way, because the way we have just described it is the *wrong* way to set up a new AdWords campaign. Creating your PPC campaign like this will cost you a lot and is unlikely to generate you much in the way of quality enquiries. Why is that? Well, there are a number of reasons.

Choosing keywords

The first problem is the choice of keywords. The issue is that there are not enough keywords and the ones that *have* been chosen are too broad.

What do we mean by keywords being too broad? Well, basically it means you are using keywords that try to target too wide an audience, including a large number of people who are not your ideal kind of customers.

If you are an estate agent in Notting Hill, most, if not all of the properties that you have on your books for sale or rental, are going to be located in Notting Hill or one of the surrounding areas such as Bayswater. So, the ideal visitor to your website is someone who is looking for an estate agent or a property for sale or rent in Notting Hill (or somewhere nearby) rather than in the more general London area.

That means, you ought to be bidding on search terms such as:

- estate agent Notting Hill
- property for sale Notting Hill

- houses for sale Notting Hill
- flats for sale Notting Hill
- real estate Notting Hill
- buy property Notting Hill
- estate agent Bayswater
- property for sale Bayswater
- houses for sale Bayswater

Admittedly there will be less people searching with those terms than there are for terms that include 'London' instead of 'Notting Hill' or 'Bayswater' but, as we said above, those people who *are* searching with these narrower criteria are far more likely to be the serious buyers who have a better idea of what it is they want to buy.

Ask yourself: would I rather talk to a hundred people a day who are not very interested in what I have to sell, or would I rather talk to ten people who know what they want to buy and know that I am the person who can sell it to them?

Anyone with any sense will opt for the ten warmer prospects and that is what you are more likely to attract if you use narrower search terms rather than broad ones.

Not only that, but it will cost you less too. Generally speaking, the broader a search term is then the more competitive it is (i.e. the more other people there are bidding on it) and hence the more expensive it is to appear high up the AdWords results for that search term.

So, in summary, tightly focused keywords mean:

- lower costs per click
- fewer clicks
- more targeted response

and hence a lower cost per sale or cost per enquiry via your website.

Writing good ad text

The second mistake that our imaginary estate agent has made in the example above is to use the wrong kind of advert. To save you going back to it, here is a reminder of what it said (minus the website address line):

> London Estate Agent
> Wide range of flats and houses
> to buy or rent. Friendly service.

The problem here is a similar one to what we saw with the keywords – it's too broad and it is not closely matched enough to the tightly focused Notting Hill and Bayswater keywords that we started to come up with just now. Why does this matter? Well, let's use an example.

Imagine you've just typed the phrase *'estate agents Brixton'* into Google and the very first advert that appears at the top of the AdWords search results is titled: "Clapham Estate Agents". The next three are all titled either "Estate Agent Brixton" or "Brixton Estate Agents".

Now, having typed *'estate agents Brixton'* into Google, you're obviously looking for an estate agent in Brixton. Whilst Clapham is only a mile or so away, you are very unlikely to click on the Clapham estate agent's advert (even though it is at the top of the list) because there are three other adverts below it which jump out and appear to match precisely what you are searching for.

So, with that principle in mind, our estate agent in Notting Hill ought to be using an advert that looks something like this instead:

> Notting Hill Estate Agent
> Estate agents in Notting Hill.
> Buying or selling? We can help.

Do you see what kind of a situation we are engineering here? Someone sits down at Google wanting to find an estate agent in Notting Hill. They type *'estate agents Notting Hill'* into Google.

Because that is one of the keywords our imaginary estate agent selected for his AdWords campaign, his advert is triggered to appear.

The potential buyer sees the advert, recognises immediately from the title that it matches what he or she is looking for, and so clicks it. If the advert had been titled "Estate Agent London" there would have been a much slimmer chance of it being clicked.

An advert that is clicked on a lot is said to have a high click-through rate (CTR). The CTR is expressed as a percentage. For example, if your advert is displayed for 100 different searches and is clicked on 14 times, then it will be said to have a CTR of 14%.

Why does this matter? Well, Google works on the theory that if an advert gets a high CTR then it must be of interest and relevance to the people who are searching. Google wants to give its users meaningful and useful search results. So it looks at the CTR and how relevant your advert is to the keywords that trigger it and it uses this to give you a Quality Score. Google then uses a combination of keyword bid price and Quality Score to determine whereabouts in the rankings a particular advert is displayed.

This means that if you have a well written advert that gets a high number of clicks then you can potentially appear higher up the listings than someone who has bid more than you but has a poorly written unfocused advert that gets fewer clicks and has a lower Quality Score.

This is a great principle because it means that small budget advertisers have the potential to compete with the big national and multi-national companies on a more level playing field. By putting in the time and effort to create carefully worded, highly relevant ads, a small retailer can potentially beat the likes of Tesco to the top spot, even though his advertising budget is a fraction of what theirs is.

Having deep pockets and trying to outbid everyone else won't necessarily get you to the top if your advert is poorly written and gets you a low Quality Score.

Matching your ads to your keywords

This leads us into the third mistake made by our imaginary estate agent. He only had one advert and one set of keywords. This is *not* the way to ensure that you always have a relevant advert with a high click-through rate.

Google refers to a group of keywords as an Ad Group. For each Ad Group you have to have at least one advert, but you can have more than that if you want. The important thing is to make sure (as we talked about just now) that each advert is relevant to the keywords.

In turn, that means that each different 'theme' you identify for your keywords needs to have its own Ad Group so as it can have its own specific advert(s).

Let's change the example and pretend to be a mortgage broker in Pimlico. The first thing we need to do is draw up a list of the areas that we want to attract new clients from. The list might look like this: Pimlico, Victoria, Chelsea, Fulham, Battersea, and Knightsbridge. This gives us the basis for our first six Ad Groups.

So, we might call our first Ad Group 'Pimlico'. This could contain keywords such as:

- Mortgage broker Pimlico
- Mortgage adviser Pimlico
- Mortgage advisor Pimlico
- Mortgage to buy flat in Pimlico

We would then need to write an advert that was specific to that group of keywords – something like:

> Mortgage Broker Pimlico
> Pimlico mortgage advisor.
> Get a quote today.

It would be a good idea to create a second advert (similar but subtly different) so as we can see over time which advert performs best. More on that later.

Then we would create an Ad Group for the next location – e.g. 'Knightsbridge'. This would have keywords such as:

- Mortgage broker Knightsbridge
- Mortgage adviser Knightsbridge
- Mortgage advisor Knightsbridge
- Mortgage advisor near Harrods

Again, we would next need to create the adverts and make them specific to those keywords For example:

> Mortgages Knightsbridge
> Knightsbridge mortgage broker
> Get a quote today.

And so on and so on……

Of course, locations are not the only variations that can be used to create Ad Groups. You can use your products as the basis for defining Ad Groups too.

For example, rather than just focusing on the term 'meat', a butcher might have one Ad Group for search terms containing beef, another for steaks, another for sausages, one for burgers, one for pork, etc.

Whatever way you decide to do it, the key thing is to keep the Ad Groups as tightly focused as possible and to make sure the ad text matches the theme of your keywords that you've used in that Ad Group.

Getting this set up can be time consuming but, as with so many things, it's the people who put in the effort who reap the rewards. There are, however, tools and shortcuts that can help you out a bit.

For example, when you are creating an ad, you can set it to automatically put the user's search terms into the title of your advert. This is called dynamic keyword insertion. It is described in detail at: **http://bit.ly/4WWCA**.

Setting your bid prices

Finding the right bid price for your keywords is going to come down a bit to trial and error and is going to depend on what product/service you are selling and what your margins are like. The three things we want to stress about bid prices are:

1. It's better to start with an easily affordable bid price and slowly increase it if required than it is to start high and lose a load of money.
2. Do not get hung up on trying to be in the top spot. Often you will find you get better click through rates and/or a better quality of visitor if your advert appears in positions 3-6 than in positions 1 and 2.
3. If you have set a reasonable bid price and yet are struggling to get on page one of the search results, then you need to look at changing your ad text and/or your keywords (or the way you have combined the two) before you go frantically ramping up your bid price. Unless you are operating in a highly competitive industry you shouldn't need to be paying several pounds per click.

Landing pages

An important, but often over-looked, part of setting up an AdWords campaign is to ensure you pick the most appropriate landing page for each of your ads. To recap, the landing page is simply the page within your website that you want someone to be taken to when they click on your advert. You do not have to send all your visitors to your site's home page and, in many cases, you would be wrong to do so.

Instead, you need to ensure you send your visitors to the page of your website which is the most relevant to what they searched for. As an example, if you had a website selling office furniture and someone searched for 'office chairs' then you would want them to go straight to the page of your website that was about office chairs when they clicked on your Google ad. Therefore, you would set this as the landing page for that particular ad.

If, on the other hand, someone searched for *'boardroom tables'* you would send them to a different landing page – one that had details of your boardroom tables.

There are two reasons why selecting the most appropriate landing page is important. Firstly, it makes life easier for your potential customer. If they land on a page which immediately gives them exactly what they want, then they are less likely to click the Back button and leave your site as soon as they've arrived (known as 'bouncing').

Secondly, the relevance of the landing page is another factor which Google uses to assess your Quality Score. And, as we know from earlier, a higher Quality Score will lead to you getting a better positioning on the Google results page for a lower cost per click.

Having covered the basics, let's take a look at some of the other things you might want to be aware of when setting up a Google AdWords campaign.

Split-testing ads

We mentioned earlier that it is a good idea to have more than one ad per Ad Group. This is so you can monitor which ad performs best and then change the one that has the lower CTR.

After a week or so, you will hopefully have enough data to be able to analyse the results and see which advert is likely to perform best in the longer term. The important figures for this are how many times each advert has been displayed and what its click-through rate is.

Armed with this information, you can then use this free utility – **www.splittester.com** – to find out whether there is any statistically significant difference in the performance of your two ads.

If one advert turns out to be noticeably weaker than the other, then you should edit the poorer performing advert and then repeat the split-testing process a couple of weeks later.

By repeating and repeating this exercise over time, you will be fine-tuning and fine-tuning your adverts until you eventually achieve the optimum possible CTR for that Ad Group. Think of it like the evolution of a species – but over a much shorter period of time!

You'd be surprised how sometimes something very minor can make a difference to the CTR of an advert. As we said earlier, the final line of your four line ad is always given over to the URL of the website you are sending people to – for example www.divadanidesign.com.

But don't forget that there are other ways you can write this URL, such as without the www. (so simply divadanidesign.com) or perhaps with some of the letters capitalised – such as www.DivadaniDesign.com for example.

From experience, doing this can often make a difference to the CTR of the ad. If you don't believe us, try it yourself. Just create an Ad Group with two adverts which are identical apart from the way you write the display URL. Have it all in lower case on one ad and have it with capitalised letters on the other. After a few days, stick the results into the Split Tester and see if there is a difference.

NOTE: By default, if you have more than one advert for an Ad Group, Google will favour the advert with the highest CTR and show that advert more often. To be able to test different ad variations properly, you need to turn off this automatic optimised ad rotation in your campaign settings and pick the option to show ads evenly.

Negative keywords

As well as setting up lists of keywords that you want your advert to appear for, you might also want to specify some keywords for which your advert definitely will *not* appear. For example, suppose you have a website selling clipart images. You might end up with a list of keywords such as: clipart images, website clipart, clipart downloads, etc.

With a list like that your advert would also be likely to appear if someone typed in other search phrases that included the term 'clipart images'. For example, your ad would probably appear if someone searched for: *'best clipart images'*. Similarly, if they searched for: *'collection of clipart images'*. This is because the search phrases include the term 'clipart images' which is a keyword you are bidding on.

That's unlikely to cause you a problem. In fact it is one of the nice things about pay-per-click that your advert will appear for related search phrases that you perhaps had not thought of and so had not bid for.

But what about if someone searches for *'free clipart images'*. Your advert will still stand a chance of being shown and clicked on. That's ok if you are actually offering free images, but yours is a site which is *selling* clipart images. So, anyone who searches for free clipart and then clicks on your ad is likely to be disappointed. And, not only that, they will also have wasted your money by clicking on your ad with no hope of being able to find what they wanted at your website.

The answer is to this problem is to use negative keywords. This simply means putting a minus sign in front of the keywords that you want your ad to *not* appear for. So, if you set up your keyword list like this:

- clipart images
- website clipart
- clipart downloads
- -free

with a minus sign in front of the word 'free', then Google would avoid showing your ad to anyone who included the word 'free' in their search term.

Square brackets and quotes

We said above that Google automatically shows your advert for related searches that you might not have explicitly included in your list of keywords. This is what Google refers to as the 'broad match' option and is the default for all keywords.

A lot of the time this is OK, but there may be times when that is not suitable. So it is important to know about how you override this. We've already talked about negative keywords, but there are two other match types you need to know about.

The first is 'phrase match' and is specified by putting your keywords in quotes. The other option is 'exact match' and this is achieved by putting your keywords in square brackets.

The differences between these options are very neatly explained at: **https://adwords.google.com/support/bin/answer.py?answer=6100**.

Conversion tracking

Once your AdWords campaign is up and running, it is important to monitor it and see if it is working for you. Failure to do this, especially in the early days of a new campaign, can result in you spending a lot of money in a very short space of time and having very little to show for it.

To get any idea of how successful your AdWords campaign is you are going to have to use conversion tracking. To do this, you first of all need to identify what the conversion goal is. In other words, when someone comes to your website, what is your ideal end result? Do you want them to make a purchase? Or download a white paper? Or fill in an enquiry form? Obviously, your goal will vary depending on what kind of website you are promoting.

For the moment, let's assume that you are a mortgage broker and that your goal is to get someone to go to your website and then fill in an enquiry form requesting that you contact them to provide them with some mortgage advice.

After the potential client has filled in your online enquiry form, they get taken to a page on your site which says something like "Thank you for your enquiry. We will be in touch very soon." It is when the potential client sees that confirmation screen that your goal can be said to have been achieved.

So, to set up conversion tracking, you just need to enable it in your AdWords account and then add a piece of code (which Google supplies) onto that confirmation page on your website – the one that people see after filling in your mortgage enquiry form.

From then on, whenever someone fills in the form, the confirmation page will send a message back to Google to tell them that a conversion has taken place.

In turn, you will then be able to view information in your AdWords account about how many of your clicks turn into enquiries (or purchases if you have a website which is selling something) and what you average cost per conversion is. You can see this information across a whole campaign or you can look at the conversion statistics for an individual Ad Group or even for an individual keyword.

By monitoring this kind of data you can tweak or get rid of any keywords that do not generate conversions or which have too high a cost per conversion. That way you can avoid getting into a situation where you are paying £5 in advertising costs for every £2 product that you sell.

For more in-depth tracking of your AdWords campaign you can, and should, link your AdWords account to your Google Analytics account so you can see more detail about what your AdWords visitors are doing once they reach your site.

Suggested action plan

- Familiarise yourself with the new form of advertising – pay-per-click.

- Spend time looking at what keywords could be used to advertise your product or service.

- Look into setting up a Google AdWords campaign. If you need help, think about employing the services of a consultant such as **www.divadanidesign.com**.

- Re-familiarise yourself with Google Analytics so you can track how traffic is being directed to your website.

- Keep testing and measuring to see how well your campaign is working.

Chapter 10

Building your brand through face-to-face marketing

Given that we are in a world of high-speed internet, complex online marketing strategies and a profusion of social media channels, it may seem strange to be talking about a form of marketing which has been around since the dawn of civilisation – pushing your product or service in a face-to-face setting.

Paradoxically though (at least on the surface), business networking is alive and well in the 21st Century. There are a whole host of business groups meeting weekly and monthly in an attempt to forge relationships and garner business leads. We have already mentioned BNI (**www.bni.eu/uk**) and 4Networking (**www.4networking.biz**), but there are other groups such as Business Referral Exchange (**www.brxnet.co.uk**) as well as all-female groups such as the Athena Network (**www.theathenanetwork.com**). There are also business organisations like the Federation of Small Businesses (**www.fsb.org.uk**) which include a variety of networking events in the package of benefits they offer to their members.

One thing all these groups and organisations have in common is that you, or a suitable representative from your company, will meet other business people in an informal setting where you will have the chance to push your VKUM (vision, key messages, USPs and mission) and potentially win new business off the back of this.

Now for some people this may seem like a torture, especially if you are expected to stand up in a room full of strangers and do a mini presentation. However, statistics show that this is one of the best and most cost effective forms of lead generation there is.

Ultimately, no matter how good your website is or how well your branding comes across, people like dealing with people. Again, it is basic animal behaviour – there's something about eye contact, seeing someone speak and reading body language that can't be replicated in any other way – even with modern video technology and high-tech websites.

To give you an idea of just how effective this is, in 2010 the 15,000 BNI members from the UK and Ireland passed £245 million worth of business - representing an average of almost £16,000 per member. Not bad given that the annual cost of attending BNI is roughly £1,000 per year - making a 16-fold return on your marketing investment.

There will of course be further costs involved in terms of the staff time you need to commit, but whichever way you look at it, face-to-face networking is very effective marketing.

Include networking in your marketing strategy

When formulating your online marketing strategy (see Chapter 7) you need to think about supplementing it with an element of offline business networking too, in order to back up what you are doing online and drive even more traffic to your website.

This networking could take several different forms, from attending seminars and conferences to running trade stands, or attending business breakfast events or social evenings. Whichever ones you or the staff within your company choose to do, you will all be ambassadors for your brand and need to present yourself as effectively as possible.

To get this right, however, you have to prepare carefully and ensure you make the best possible impression.

Do your research

Whatever event you wish to attend, you need to do your homework beforehand. Many networking groups will have their own websites that list all the members who attend regularly, along with their contact details. Even at seminars or conferences, it is often possible to get a pretty good understanding of who will be attending – particularly those companies who are taking stands.

Where possible, try to contact people you may be interested in talking to beforehand and set up a one-to-one meeting with them. You could also try posting a message on LinkedIn or Twitter asking if anyone is attending the event.

You are trying to meet not only potential clients, but also people who could be good introducers for you. Thus, if you are an interior designer then architects, builders and estate agents would fall into this category. Similarly, if you're a florist then event organisers, wedding planners and photographers would make excellent introducers.

With every person you are hoping to meet, either look at their website or check out their LinkedIn profile. This will enable you to understand a little more about them so you can get more out of any initial meeting.

Business cards and email signatures

The humble business card has its origins in the 17th Century when they were used by tradesmen to advertise their wares. However, four centuries later, they still have a vital role to play in business communications. Whether printed on paper or sent electronically, a business card can convey a huge amount of information about your company or products.

Ideally, a business card should include all of the following:

- Usual contact details
- Details of your website and any relevant social media pages
- Direct URL for your own LinkedIn profile
- A clear vision statement or strapline for your company on the back
- Good branding

It should also be laid out very simply as there are now many business card readers on the market – whether as apps for your phone or as mini-scanners which plug into your PC. The easier your business card is to read, the simpler it is for someone to download the information from it.

In fact, your email signature should contain all of the above information too. That way, each time you send an email, you're conveying your key brand messages and helping to drive traffic to your website.

Think about your VKUM

As with any form of marketing, whether talking to people on a one-to-one level or as an audience, you need to remember your VKUM. And the more refined you make it, the easier it will be for anyone listening to you to understand what it is you do.

It is worth writing down each of the elements of your VKUM on a small slip of paper and keeping this with you when you are out networking. For example, if you are a web designer in Norwich, your VKUM could be written out as follows:

- **What is your vision?**
  Creating affordable sites fit for the social media age.

- **What key messages do you want to convey?**
  - o   Norwich-based but work right across East Anglia
  - o   Specialise in branding, design, web development and social media implementation
  - o   Long track record of working in the retail sector
  - o   Affordable but high quality

- **USP**
  We can design and build high quality social media platforms i.e. making your Twitter page look like your website and enhancing the spec of your Facebook page.

- **What is the mission statement for your product or brand?**
  To deliver high quality but cost effective websites that will provide your company with the right online platform to generate new business and build your brand. Based in the centre of Norwich, our team includes specialists in branding, design, web development and social media so we can cater for any online marketing requirement you may have.

Presentation skills

For many of us, standing up in a room full of people can be a daunting prospect. However, even those people who are comfortable at public speaking need to have prepared beforehand to ensure they come across as professionally as possible.

If you are speaking at a seminar, presenting a workshop at an event or standing in front of a networking group, it is always a good idea to have done some form of dress run, whether to your colleagues or even into a mirror – you'd be surprised what you may find out about yourself from this exercise.

Clearly there are common sense issues to bear in mind such as dressing in an appropriate manner for the occasion, having a glass of water to hand during your presentation and ensuring that any marketing collateral you may have – be it hard copy or electronic – is working properly.

If you really do have a fear about speaking in public, there are a range of different solutions from seeking advice from NLP practitioners and hypnotherapists through to attending presentational skills workshops (something offered for all new members joining BNI).

Alternatively, if you have colleagues or business partners who are better suited to presenting, it would of course be better to let them do the talking.

Join a networking organisation

Originally an American idea, networking groups have sprung up all over the UK. There are now a range of different ways in which business owners can interface with each other. There is the formalised setting of BNI, traditional meetings, or more ad hoc groups such as 'tweetups' – a gathering of Twitter users who meet face-to-face over coffee.

The beauty of having so many different types of networking groups is that you should pretty much be able to find one which fits around your work schedule. For example, many BNI meetings start at 07:15 and are over by 08:30, meaning you take almost no time out of your usual working day. Alternatively, some people prefer to go to evening drinks events when they may feel more relaxed.

Traditional

Many organisations will hold events, whether they be seminars, dinners or presentations. This can be a great way to meet fellow local businesses. Both the Federation of Small Businesses and Chambers of Commerce (**www.britishchambers.org.uk**) will have local branches you can join. Most events will be held in the evening and there will usually be a nominal charge to cover expenses.

Formal

BNI is the most successful networking organisation in the world. In the UK and Ireland alone there are well over 600 chapters in operation meaning that there will probably be one close to you, whether you are in the most rural part of Cornwall or in the heart of Merseyside. Check **www.bni.eu/uk** to find out more.

The philosophy of BNI is givers gain – a principle not far removed from *what goes around, comes around*. Within the organisation, the idea is that the more business leads and referrals you pass to members of your group, the more business you will get in return.

The key thing about BNI is that wherever you go in the UK (and indeed the world, as BNI is in 55 different countries around the globe from Australia to Zimbabwe and from Luxembourg to China), every meeting will be run in exactly the same way, using a script which has been developed over the past 25 years to maximise the amount of business which can be done in a 75-minute timeframe.

Furthermore, each chapter is run along the same lines as a business. It has a management team, it sets goals, it monitors performance and it aims for growth. This means that the responsibility is very much on members to ensure they are performing to the best of their ability by bringing referrals, inviting along visitors or giving a testimonial for another person within the group.

There is also an expectation that people attend meetings once a week, or at least send a substitute if they cannot make it. The reasoning behind this is that you are trying to build relationships with a collection of other business people and, to do so, you need to have visibility. You should think of the rest of the group as colleagues. If you were working in a real business, would your colleagues think it acceptable for you not to show up for work every day?

BNI is not just about referrals though. As in the business world, there are also opportunities for members to improve their skills as BNI puts on regular training sessions on how to be a better networker, how to become a more polished presenter, and how to refer more business.

Very often, this may be the most cost effective way of meeting your continuing professional development requirements and is, in itself, a great way to network with other business professionals.

As we mentioned before, there are other formal networking groups such as 4Networking, BRX and Athena. These will have more or less structured agendas and hold regular meetings. Many will have a strong online as well as offline presence, allowing members to continue the process of networking before and after meetings, which is key.

Informal

Unsurprisingly, considering the growth of LinkedIn and Twitter, there are dozens of groups that meet informally around the UK. In a not dissimilar way from online dating, business owners get to know each other online and will then meet once a week for coffee or drinks to carry forward the conversation in the real environment.

Illustrating how social media and networking are now starting to cross over, the face-to-face meetings can quickly prove the worth of spending time updating social networking sites and seeking out potential new clients/introducers.

Towns like Tunbridge Wells have very active online communities and as a result there are two networking groups – Twuttle which meets on Wednesday mornings and Twuddle which meets fortnightly on Tuesday evenings (**http://twuttle.com/about**). The advantage of these is that networking can go on almost uninterrupted as conversations continue online or offline. They can also prove to be a valuable support network for people who are sole traders.

Roger Purdie (@bookkeepingRog), is a book-keeper based in the town who is also a member of BNI (**www.bni-tunbridgewells.com**). He has met numerous new clients via Twuttle as well as acting as an introducer for both his BNI chapter and other businesses in the town.

In addition, there are a multitude of profession-based groups which are springing up. Whether it be therapists, creative people or tradesmen, they all serve the same purpose – to provide an environment to share best practice, to network and build both contacts and brand. Simply type 'business networking' and the name of your geographical location into a search engine and you'll quickly find a group close to you.

When choosing a group to join, you have to weigh up a number of different factors such as:

- Cost
- Investment of time
- Likely return on your investment
- Whether the people there will be able to introduce you to contacts within your target markets
- How often you need to attend
- Proximity to your place of work or home

Like any other form of marketing, you need to test and measure the effectiveness of your networking to make sure you are getting the best value for money. There may be some instances when you stop networking and invest in other forms of marketing (e.g. Google AdWords) as a way to generate new business leads.

It is always worth trying out a number of different networking groups to see which one will work best for you. Even within BNI and the other UK-wide organisations, you need to do the due diligence in deciding which of their many chapters/local groups could be of most benefit to you and your business.

Building relationships

All face-to-face networking is about building sustainable relationships. It is NOT about trying to extract as much business from people as you can. This is the difference between hunters and farmers and it is important to note the distinction between the two.

Hunters will be the people who attend as many different networking groups as they can, picking up as many business cards and contacts as possible and then trying to sell directly to them or even spamming them with the services they provide.

Farmers on the other hand will be people who try to cultivate the contacts they have made over weeks, months, or even years in some cases. From having regular meetings with other members within their group or networking circle, to offering free business advice and support, these people will work hard to establish credibility in their local area. As a result, over time, they will be in a position to benefit from the goodwill and contacts they have built up.

Therefore whether you attend an FSB meeting or go as a visitor to a BNI Chapter, this should be seen as just the start. It is no different from going on a date – even if it's love at first sight, you still won't know the person until you've been on a number of dates with them.

With this in mind, it is important to be as proactive as you can but do NOT try to sell directly to people. If you are a member of BNI, do attend your Chapter every single week. At the same time, do not limit yourself to one circle of contacts. There are BNI chapters all over the country and you are always welcome go to one as a visitor. Also, the more different networking organisations you attend, the larger your circle of contacts and the more chance you have of referring business to people within your network and, of course, winning new business yourself.

There is a definite networking mentality which you can develop. Whenever you are seeing clients, visiting friends/family or even when you go to a shop/hotel/restaurant, it is a good idea to keep your eyes and ears open for possible new business leads – not simply for yourself but also for those people within your sphere of influence.

For example, imagine you are an office supply rep who has a good working relationship with a florist in your networking group. When visiting a large firm in the centre of Manchester to deliver a new set of office furniture, you notice there are expensive-looking floral displays on the front desk. Instead of ignoring them, you find out from the receptionist who supplies them and ask if the company would be willing to try out other suppliers.

That's how networking should work. You are not seeking any immediate material advantage for yourself because you know that, somewhere down the line, the florist may handle the flowers at a wedding where they find out the father of the bride runs a company that needs to overhaul all their office furniture.

However, for you and the florist to get to the stage where you are happy to 'sell in' your networking colleagues, you need to have spent time getting to understand who they are and how their businesses work.

This is why regular one-on-one meetings are always a great idea. Usually they happen after networking meetings but a good idea is to have them at each other's place of work – that way you can understand the other person's work environment and meet their colleagues.

In most networking organisations, you never really start to get business referrals until you have sat down with the majority of people within your group. It's a credibility issue. Just because you see someone once a week and hear them speak for a minute or so, doesn't mean you would recommend them to a client or friend. You have to get to know them.

This is where testimonials are so important. Obviously, the more recommendations you can get from people within a networking group, the more credible you will become and the more likely you are to get referred business leads.

Again, there is a connection between offline and online networking. If you have a fully updated profile on LinkedIn, along with lots of recommendations from former colleagues or clients, this will help to build your credibility much faster than without having this resource. At the same time, if you do a good job within your networking group, you would hopefully get a written testimonial from that person, which you could put onto your LinkedIn profile – thus building your brand and reputation online too.

Becoming more profitable

As you build an ever-expanding set of online and offline contacts, new business leads will start to find you rather than the other way round. If you have built up a solid network of followers on Twitter and connections on LinkedIn, and you regularly attend face-to-face networking meetings and seminars, you will be maximising your visibility and ensuring that you have the best possible chance of being referred new business.

At the same time, you could also become a very useful person to know, bringing you into a type of matchmaking role, where you bring together interested parties who could end up doing business with each other. Potentially you could even earn money out of this in introduction fees, depending on the nature of the relationship you have.

Earlier on we referred to the importance of having a good website to underpin your social media activity. Your website is equally important to the success of your face-to-face meetings. Generally, the first thing someone will do after receiving your business card is to look at your website and/or your LinkedIn profile to see if these back up what you were talking about. Next time you go to a networking meeting or attend a conference, check your website analytics in the days that follow to see how many people have visited your site as a result.

No matter how good you are at promoting your brand in person, if your website and social media don't stack up, you will potentially miss out on the new business. By the same token, if someone in your networking group recommends you to a third party and your online marketing is not up to scratch, the lead is very likely to go cold.

Thus, no matter how proactive you are in person, it is imperative that you back this up online by updating blogs and social media sites.

Suggested action plan

- Find out about available networking opportunities in your area.

- Attend a number of these groups to ascertain which one is likely to be of most benefit to your business.

- If you don't feel confident as the 'face' of your business, either look out for professional training or see if anyone else within your organisation could take that role.

- Build up relationships with a wide circle of people and businesses. Do not restrict yourself solely to people who you think could directly benefit you. Cultivate 'off the wall' contacts – you never know who could bring you your next lead.

- Attend networking meetings regularly and try to have one-to-one meetings with key people within your group or chapter.

- Be as proactive as you can both offline and online.

Chapter 11

Creating a social media culture

Earlier in the book, we spoke about how there has been a democratisation in the way that people and businesses communicate with the outside world. Instead of having to rely on third party organisations such as newspapers, TV and radio (still very much the norm in many parts of the world even today), we all now have the power to become broadcasters and media players ourselves.

With this power comes responsibility though. Fleet Street, the TV stations and the wealth of other publications all have to abide by various codes of conducts, Government statutes, and laws governing what they can or cannot broadcast. This is to ensure the stability of the country, protection of its citizens and to prevent people or companies making claims that are false or inaccurate (particularly with regard to adverts).

Therefore, there is obviously a degree of concern that the world of blogs and social media side-steps this security cordon. Given the furore over Wikileaks seemingly able to publish sensitive data about governments almost at will, this is something that needs to be looked at closely by large corporations and also security services who are now called upon to wage more of a cyber than a physical war against outside threats.

That said, there are still numerous checks and balances in place to ensure that ordinary citizens, organisations and companies don't have their reputations sullied and there isn't illegal placement or promotion of products online. For example, as of March 2011, the Advertising Standards Authority (**www.asa.org.uk**), became responsible for overseeing marketing communications on companies' own websites and in other third party web space under their control (e.g. Facebook and Twitter). Content placed on these internet marketing channels now has to comply with advertising rules set out in the Committee of Advertising Practice (CAP) Code (**http://www.cap.org.uk/The-Codes/CAP-Code.aspx**).

This means that all companies must now ensure that the marketing messages they put on their websites and use in social media are legal, decent, honest and truthful. Businesses are encouraged to make sure their websites comply by seeking help and advice from the ASA.

At the same time, there are also ways to ensure that you can prevent your brand or reputation being lowered and there are specialist law firms (such as **www.azrights.co.uk**) who can assist you. Social media accounts can be shut down and internet service providers (ISPs) can be forced to disclose the details of people who are deemed to be mounting campaigns of defamation.

In addition, many corporations are now using specialist PR and online communications agencies to ensure that not only is their reputation protected in the mainstream traditional media, but it is also monitored in the blogosphere and on social media channels.

What does this mean, though, for owners of small businesses and how can you both leverage this new-found media clout whilst at the same time protecting your brand and reputation?

Everyone has a marketing role to play

Up until now, marketing was put fairly and squarely into the hands of either marketing managers or, if it were an SME, the business owner. Therefore any key decisions about how the product or brand was going to be presented were taken by a fairly small group of people.

Taking a local authority as an example, the traditional model of marketing would involve a head of marketing making strategic decisions about where to invest its marketing budget – publications, customer relations, media relations, public relations, newsletters, etc. Where applicable, marketing and communications professionals would be used either in-house or as external consultants to achieve these marketing aims.

At the same time, each department would have their own separate remit – customer relations to deal with council stakeholders directly; media relations and public relations to deal both reactively and proactively with the media; marketing to promote products and services directly to people living and working within the local authority area.

Now, however, there needs to be much closer working between departments as they have become inter-related as never before. In the new social media arena, there is a direct link between customer relations, media relations, public relations and even internal communications and human resources. Instead of having two key mouthpieces – council publications and the press office – there are potentially hundreds, in the shape of individual members of staff.

Even in much smaller organisations, everyone now has the potential to assist in the marketing of your product or service. For example, we have already mentioned how it is worth training up one of the younger members of your team to become the 'social media champion' for your company.

However, there is no reason why all the other members of staff cannot also contribute to pushing your brand. We have already mentioned how all personnel should have LinkedIn pages, complete with a cohesive mission statement for your company and a link to the company website included in their profiles. In addition, everyone should have a similar email signature and, where applicable, they should be encouraging as many of their friends and family as possible to 'Like' the company Facebook page, follow it on Twitter, and even add the company's YouTube channel to their favourites.

Moving to a deeper level though, to have the best chance of publicising your brand and enhancing the profiles of individual members of staff, you need to create a particular kind of culture within your organisation – a culture of openness, a willingness to promote the brand, and networking.

This is not dissimilar to how public relations has traditionally worked and, in fact, any incumbent PR agency could be brought in to assist with this new role. Traditionally, PR consultants or in-house press officers would act as news editors, working with marketing managers and key individuals within organisations to provide a steady flow of salient information which they could work with and sell to the media. This would result in press releases being prepared and coverage then (hopefully) appearing.

Depending on the brief, PR consultants would be asked to promote a specific brand or service. To do so, though, they would need to have case studies, research and statistics to help back up the story – just as a journalist would need when writing a news story.

Thus, if you were being asked to promote a chain of pubs, you'd be looking for examples of happy customers, launches of new product lines (e.g. guest beers, new menus, refurbished pubs, etc) and perhaps a survey on customer service. The agency would then work to place these stories with the applicable press – trade, local or even broadcast media.

However, there have always been a number of stories that weren't quite interesting enough for the press but would be relevant enough to be used in other forms of marketing such as newsletters, brochures, direct mail, etc. This is exactly the sort of material which can now be given centre stage on blogs and social media platforms.

Using the news editor analogy, in an ideal world, everyone within your organisation could act as a virtual reporter, providing information that may be of use for your news page or social media sites. Let's use a building firm as an example of how this could work in practice:

- Daily updates on the sort of jobs being carried out by the firm – again stressing the company's key messages
- Links to the websites or Linked profiles of any suppliers that are used
- If working for a company, mention their website
- Focus on the specialisations of individual members of the workforce e.g. knowledge of listed properties, working with lime mortar or sustainable materials
- Publicising positive testimonials from current/previous customers

- Human interest-type updates – e.g. out-of-the-ordinary jobs, rescuing cats from lofts, staff being promoted/ getting married, etc
- New product lines appearing on the market

In this case study, all members of the firm would feed these bits of information to one person who would then put it all up online.

It is important, however, that you get buy-in to what you are trying to achieve from the majority of people within your organisation. It is all very well having the vision and drive, but without assistance from your colleagues it is akin to having a fantastic recipe but no ingredients.

One of the indirect positive outcomes from this is that one or two members of the team get a chance to expand their roles within the organisation. Therefore office managers or secretaries can learn new skills and build their knowledge about new media, so they not only assist the company but also further their own career.

Redefining corporate guidelines

Too many organisations currently have a negative view of social media. Many companies prevent employees from being able to access any sites like Facebook or Twitter, based on the premise that time spent on these sites is time not being spent on company business. This argument has been used over and over again – first with the introduction of computers in the 1980s and then with the arrival of email and the web in the 1990s.

While a minority of staff undoubtedly will always abuse the privilege of having a PC at work, the majority will carry on with their work regardless. Also, as we are now in an era of mobile internet, any employees who are hell-bent on updating their Facebook status on a regular basis will carry on doing it on their smartphones anyway.

Therefore, the IT, human resources and marketing managers should all work together to develop new corporate guidelines on how an organisation communicates with the outside world. This holds as true for a small business as it does for a large local authority or charity.

1. Access to social media sites

Review the current level of access that staff have to social networks. If you have a policy of blocking all these sites, look again at your personnel and ascertain how many have access to mobile internet via their smartphones. Also try to identify which members of staff could be used as online 'news editors'. To turn a potential negative into a positive, if there are people you think may be abusing the system by being on Facebook all day, you could give them the task of updating the corporate page, thereby utilising their social media skills and legitimising their presence online.

If there are real concerns about staff abusing their time at work by constantly updating social media, this should be addressed in the same way as you would if they were always late, off sick, or not achieving the objectives set out for them. Every company has its fair share of time-wasters and they will always find ways of not doing what they are told.

2. Use of social media sites

For those companies who do allow access to Facebook, Twitter, YouTube and LinkedIn, it is important to lay down guidelines on what staff can or cannot do. You do want as wide a spread of staff as possible to contribute to building your brand, but it is important to retain a uniform corporate identity.

LinkedIn – as previously stated, all applicable members of staff should have up-to-date profiles on the site, complete with a previously agreed mission statement for the organisation. Where possible, any status updates should be linked to the company's corporate Twitter profile.

Staff must also recognise that while they are working as

employees of the company, they should uphold the company ethos and should not damage the brand in any way. Any updates must also have a business connotation and must not be seen as a personal communications tool or as a way to find alternative employment.

Facebook – all staff who have personal profiles on the site MUST make sure they are only visible to friends. Unfortunately the younger generation are not careful about maintaining their online security and as a result many of their profiles are visible to all of Facebook's 550 million users.

You need to appoint someone to be the named administrator of your Facebook page. This means they will have full access to the site and will be able to update it from a phone as well as a PC, so they must be aware of the responsibility. To use a journalistic phrase, "everything you say should be taken as being 'on the record'".

Do invite staff to 'Like' the corporate page but there should be no compulsion to do so, except initially to get the required 25 fans to have a branded Facebook username.

Finally, make staff aware that they should be very careful if they wish to make defamatory remarks about the company on their personal Facebook pages as this is no different from publishing such statements in an offline publication.

Twitter – encourage certain key staff to have their own dedicated Twitter pages. For example, PR consultant Fiona Brandhorst, working for London PR agency Wriglesworth, has **www.twitter.com/FionaBrandhorst** as her Twitter account, through which she is not only promoting herself, but her employer too. This could be useful in a multi-disciplined firm where partners need to push their own brand or service. Clearly, they need to make sure it is properly branded, links through to their specific page on the company website, and contains their key messages.

Similarly with franchised companies, individual franchisees could initially set up their LinkedIn profiles to update the main Twitter site before setting up their own sub-branded Twitter profiles.

However, as with Facebook, all employees should be aware that defamatory remarks may come back to haunt them, so caution should be exercised before making potentially inflammatory updates.

Other social media – employees need to be made aware that while they are free to comment on personal blogs, social media sites and forums with their own thoughts and views, they need to take care about what they say in case it could be seen as being detrimental to their employer's brand. For example, if a shop assistant worked in a butchers and blogged about how much they hated eating red meat, it could undermine the brand.

3. **HR policy and social media relations**

HR managers need to look at existing contracts for staff and consider updating contracts for new joiners to reflect the changing nature of corporate communications. With all members of staff having access to an unlimited audience via the internet, it is important that guidelines are laid down about what they can or cannot talk about as employees.

Clearly the capacity for leaks is greater than ever, making the work of a traditional-style press office or marketing team more difficult, so management needs to be aware of this and have procedures in place to combat any threats which could be posed as a result.

One way to deal with this issue, and indeed to find out about any potentially harmful online mentions about your firm, is to set up Google Alerts (**www.google.com/alerts**). You need to have an account set up with Google to do this, but it is free. With Alerts, you put in the relevant keywords and you will then receive an email every time they are mentioned. Essentially this can act as a free online press monitoring service.

Of course, you can always simply put the name of your organisation into any search engines to see what comes up. The key thing is to deal with any threats rather than hope they will go away. Therefore you need to open a dialogue (preferably offline) with whoever is bad-mouthing you and discover what issue it is they have with your company – this goes for whether or not they are an employee.

At the same time, you can set up saved searches within Twitter with your company name. You can therefore check regularly to see if you are being mentioned negatively (or indeed positively) in any Twitter updates and act accordingly. One response could involve replying to the offending tweet(s) with an open suggestion to contact you. Or you could reply with a short statement contained within a shortened hyperlink using a service like **www.bit.ly**.

With both Twitter and Facebook, if you believe that someone is conducting a campaign of harassment or defamation, you can report this to the administrators who have the authority to remove the perpetrator's account.

Finally, you can also put your company name into the search bar of Facebook to check whether anyone has set up a group or page which may be injurious to your company brand or reputation. As with the point above, under certain circumstances you can get these taken off the site. Alternatively, though, you can join the group or 'Like' the page and enter into an open dialogue with the creator – in essence this gives you a right of reply like hotels have with TripAdvisor.

4. **Taking care of customers**

Leading on from this last point, if your customers have a legitimate concern or complaint about your company or the service/product you have provided, they may choose to voice this online via social media and blogs, rather than contacting you directly.

It is now commonplace for disgruntled customers to post something onto Twitter or Facebook, whether they are complaining about their hotel room, flight or evening meal. And, with mobile internet platforms, people are complaining real time so it is vital that you are closely monitoring the internet at all times – especially if you know there is a problem. For example, in the run-up to Christmas 2010 there were unprecedented falls of snow which prevented many online retailers being able to deliver. These companies, as well as trying to find ways around the problem, should have been regularly updating online sites to inform their customers as to what was happening.

The key is establishing lines of communication. If customers feel they aren't being listened to, it makes them more likely to complain and more likely to give your product or service a bad name.

In many larger organisations with a customer service department, it would be beneficial for managers to meet with whoever is updating the online and social media accounts so that they are kept informed about any potentially difficult situations or customers who may have an axe to grind.

This is no different from traditional media relations except that, in the old days, disgruntled customers would have gone directly to a newspaper or perhaps written a letter to the editor. Now they may decide to use social media as a soap box. In extreme cases, people have even set up websites with a similar domain name to the company they are unhappy with (another reason to register a wide set of domain names relevant to the company).

As with media relations, you need to have a prepared, corporate 'line to take' which will include an outline of the problem, examples of what you are doing to rectify it and perhaps details of possible compensation you will be offering.

Going back to the snow example mentioned earlier, if you were an online toy retailer, you should have updated your website and social media sites on a regular basis with weather reports, the latest news on the roads, and links to various courier company websites and sites such as **www.bbc.co.uk/news**. In this way you could have at least kept your customers informed as to what was going on.

Moving forward, and given the possibility that deliveries would no longer be made before Christmas, a well-prepared statement should have been put on your website giving full details about the difficulties posed by the weather, your policy with regards to refunds, and recommendations for getting hold of the toys through other means.

As a result, despite your customers not getting their toys in time for Christmas, your reputation would have been unlikely to suffer and you may indeed have engendered a degree of customer loyalty in recognition of the steps you had taken to communicate with people directly.

To be able to do this though, there need to be clear internal lines of communication. If one part of the organisation does not talk to another, that's when problems start. To give an example, during 2008 and 2009, many newspaper property sections were covering a new way of purchasing property – part-buy/part-rent, where you bought a percentage of a property then paid subsidised rent to a housing association for the remainder. It was pitched as the cool and trendy way to buy property, at a time when getting on the property ladder was deemed unaffordable.

Editors were initially sceptical about running stories, but with greater and greater numbers of middle class professionals buying in this manner, journalists were assigned to write stories. But to make the stories stand up, the reporters needed case studies of exactly this type of demographic. Unfortunately, as many housing associations did not have an adequate after-sales service, many potential case studies were unhappy with their property they had bought so could not be used in any article. Therefore, in this case, a PR story was directly and adversely affected by badly working customer relations departments.

It is interesting to note that, even today, despite a huge proportion of potential part-buy/part-rent clients being on social media, most housing associations will not have a presence on social networking sites for fear of the negative comments that will be posted. They are thus missing out on a potentially huge audience of people because they do not want to sort out their customer service.

Suggested action plan

- Put together a set of guidelines for staff about social media.

- Establish which staff could be trained up as 'social media officers' within your organisation.

- Create an environment where everyone is in a position to contribute to your marketing.

- If applicable, prepare yourself for negative comments online and have procedures in place to deal with them.

- Monitor what is being said about you online.

- Have open and direct communication channels to your customers.

Chapter 12

Next steps

We have covered a huge amount of ground in this book, from the history of the internet to new forms of advertising and the exponential growth of social networking sites. For those of you who are new to the world of online marketing, this is a huge amount of information to take on board in one go.

At the end of every chapter, we have put together a simple list of bullet points. Our advice would be to use these as a starting point. Certainly don't try and implement them all at once or you will be overwhelmed.

There are of course hundreds of books, blogs and forums about virtually every topic that we have covered here. Once you have familiarised yourself with the new landscape, a useful next step would be to earmark areas that you would like more information on and then use these additional resources to continue learning.

Keep re-educating yourself

One of the key drivers to this new form of marketing is the huge advance in technology. Innovations are now happening at such a rapid rate that anyone involved with marketing has to spend part of their time constantly re-educating themselves.

For example, by looking at the web analytics for many companies, it is possible to see the huge growth in people viewing websites from mobile internet browsers. While for many websites, only 5-6% of traffic will be coming in this way, when viewed year-on-year, you would expect to see a five-fold increase in people browsing sites using iPhones, Blackberries or Android phones before too long.

Furthermore, while we have highlighted the key social networking sites – Facebook, Twitter, YouTube and LinkedIn – and how they are growing almost exponentially, there is no reason why they themselves could not one day be eclipsed by a new player which is yet to emerge. Sites such as Zorpia (**www.zorpia.com**), Tumblr (**www.tumblr.com**) and Quora (**www.quora.com**) are just three new players in the market.

It is not inconceivable that some of the sites may merge one day or that one of them may grow to become almost ubiquitous – something Facebook seems to be doing very well at presently.

Website design and search marketing are also constantly evolving, with new ideas and methods emerging on an almost daily basis.

One area of certainty, though, is that if you do not keep pace with these technological advances, or if you stick your head in the sand, there is a real risk that your competitors WILL adapt, thereby leaving you at a commercial disadvantage. So doing nothing is NOT an option!

Read books, blogs and social media

Being proactive in business is one of the most vital skills to have. A thirst for knowledge, a willingness to adapt and learn new practices, as well as being prepared to channel your resources into new areas, will help you stay ahead of the game when it comes to fusion marketing.

If you go to Amazon and type any of the topics we have covered in this book into the search facility, you will see a huge range of publications. Some recommended titles are:

- The New Rules of Marketing and PR – David Meerman Scott
- The E-myth Revisited – Michael Gerber
- The Long Tail – Chris Anderson
- What Would Google Do? – Jeff Jarvis
- Inbound Marketing: Get Found Using Google, Social Media and Blogs – Brian Halligan and Dharmesh Shah
- How to Make Your Communication Stick – Andy Bounds
- Networking Like a Pro: Turning Contacts into Connections – Ivan Misner

There are also some useful blogs and websites which you might want to follow:

- **www.hubspot.com**
- **www.econsultancy.com**
- **www.inboundmarketingblog.com**
- **www.socialmediaexaminer.com**
- **www.mashable.com**

If you are interested in online forums, these are particularly appropriate for small businesses:

- **www.ukbusinessforum.co.uk**
- **www.businesszone.co.uk**

Of course, other ways to update your knowledge base include following marketing consultants on Twitter (e.g. the authors – @2010mediauk and @davidmiles – or @DivadaniLtd), following people in similar industries to yours on Twitter, and joining groups on LinkedIn who talk about online marketing – such as Social Media Influence or Thoseinmedia.

This book also has its own Twitter page (**www.twitter.com/fusionthebook**) plus a Facebook page (**wwww.facebook.com/fusionbook**) which will give readers the chance to interact with the authors, learn up-to-date information and ask questions.

Face-to-face networking, as well as being a great way to build your brand, can also be used as a way to meet contacts who can help educate you.

Finally, for those of you who would like cost effective training on the issues outlined within this book, **www.businesstrainingmadesimple.co.uk** runs training courses in London on all aspects of online marketing.

Identifying marketing specialists to help you

Throughout the book we have referred to many distinctive areas of marketing, whether it be web design, branding or search marketing. Clearly there is a need to find the best specialists in your area who can provide you with a cost effective service.

As outlined in Chapter 8 when we talked about finding web designers, it is important to use both your offline and online networks to find these companies or consultants. Putting a request onto LinkedIn and/or Twitter can be the first stage e.g. *looking for #web #designers in #Hertfordshire* or *restaurant in #Bucks seeks #branding #consultant.*

For some companies, it is important to find specialists who are close to you. This may be because you want to build up a face-to-face rapport with them, it makes it easier to hold meetings, or because you like doing business locally. This is where face-to-face networking can come into its own. Speak to your contacts or people at the networking events and ask them to refer you to anyone they have used or would recommend.

Once you have some names, look at their websites and social media pages to gain an understanding of who they are and what they do. They may well list some of their past or current clients – you could even contact them directly to ascertain what service they have received.

Clearly it is important to do your homework. Many businesses fall into the trap of using the first person or organisation who contacts them and not doing proper due diligence. The other pitfall is using 'friends of friends' who, on the surface seem cheap but are not up to the job. This is particularly true for web design.

Search marketing

One of the primary aims of this book is to explain how you can attract more customers. We have spoken about the three main ways to direct leads to your website – 'organic' traffic (social media, traditional marketing, word of mouth, blogs, etc), search engine optimisation and pay-per-click advertising.

Moving forward, you'll need to think about which of these are most applicable to your business as well as looking at the amount of time each of these may involve.

Blogging and updating social media may be free, but to do them properly may take up large amounts of time. On the other hand, getting a specialist to run an AdWords campaign might require a moderate financial investment but would free up you and/or your staff to get on with running your business.

And finally......

Remember that although a revolution is taking place which is continuing to transform the way we communicate, many of the age-old rules of doing business still apply: people will always want to deal with other people, success breeds success, word of mouth referrals and testimonials 'sell' your business better than you can, and it is important to get your marketing right. The main difference today is the way technology can be applied to supercharge these rules and give them a modern twist.

If you only take one thing from this book, though, it must be the need to have an adequate strategy. At a recent social media training seminar we ran, over 80% of the small businesses attending had no dedicated marketing plan. If you want to thrive in the new media age, you need to ensure *your* business is in the other 20%.

Use this book as the basis for creating and developing your fusion marketing strategy.

We wish you well!

The Sheffield College

Norton LRC
Telephone: 0114 260 2334

David Taylor

David has over 18 years experience of the UK media scene garnered from a career in journalism, in-house media relations, PR and marketing consultancy. This includes media management, campaign implementation, marketing and communications strategy as well as online marketing and social media expertise.

Educated at the University of Aberystwyth and holding a BSc Econ in International Relations, David received professional training as a journalist with the National Council for the Training of Journalists (NCTJ) in 1993.

His past employers have included local newspapers, the planning profession, London Transport, the Millennium Dome, national estate agent Strutt & Parker and Adventis Group.

David set up 2010media in 2009 in response to the fragmentation of the media in the UK along with the resultant explosion in 'new media' – especially blogs and social networking sites like Twitter, Facebook, YouTube and LinkedIn. His clients now include hotels, estate agents, property developers, law firms, business start-ups and charities.

A member of the Chartered Institute of Public Relations (CIPR), David has run online marketing seminars for a number of organisations including the Hotel Booking Agents Association (HBAA), Business Networking International (BNI) as well as the National Housing Federation (NHF). He also runs regular seminars with David Miles for Business Training Made Simple in London.

David is also very active within BNI where he is currently an Assistant Director for the London North Central Region. His role is to help members to get the best out of face-to-face networking through training and mentoring.

David is married and lives with his wife Jenny, along with their sons Felix and Jack plus two cats, in Kent.

David Miles

David set up his first business in 1996, at the age of 19, providing IT consultancy services to clients such as Shell, BT, and Diageo. Today he is a director of Divadani Ltd, a company which he co-founded in 2004.

Divadani provides internet marketing training and consultancy, Google AdWords pay-per-click advertising management, and internet lead generation services to businesses across the UK and Europe.

Despite his technical background, David is good at explaining things in plain English. Consequently, a lot of his work at Divadani involves delivering group training, as well as working with clients on a one-to-one basis in order to understand their business goals and then identify how the web can help them achieve the results they want.

Over the past few years David has been a regular presenter and trainer at various seminars and workshops, ranging from short introductions to how businesses can make effective use of the web and social media, through to full day courses on using Google AdWords to increase profits.

Aside from running his own business, David also serves on the board of directors of the Federation of Small Businesses (FSB), the UK's leading business organisation, and is a member of the FSB's National IT Committee with responsibility for helping determine the organisation's online marketing strategy.

David is a strong advocate of small business and entrepreneurship, and in 2010 was awarded an Honorary Fellowship of the Institute of Enterprise and Entrepreneurs in recognition of his contribution to enterprise in the UK.

David lives in Essex with his wife, Jane, their two young children, Sophie and Alfie, and a highly strung cat.

Lightning Source UK Ltd.
Milton Keynes UK
UKOW050718281212

204152UK00005B/156/P